THE MYSTERY OF THE GOLDEN CHEST

● ● ● ●

Joy and Tragedy in Lives Connected
to the Ark and Its Contents

Doris Irish Lacks

Dear Irene and Dewan,

Love and blessings.

Cousin Doris

TEACH Services, Inc.
P U B L I S H I N G
www.TEACHServices.com ● (800) 367-1844

Copyright © 2019 Doris Irish Lacks
Copyright © 2019 TEACH Services, Inc.
ISBN-13: 978-1-4796-0993-2 (Paperback)
ISBN-13: 978-1-4796-0994-9 (ePub)
Library of Congress Control Number: 2018962314

Published by

TEACH Services, Inc.
P U B L I S H I N G
www.TEACHServices.com • (800) 367-1844

IN MEMORY

● ● ● ●

Walter Lacks, the patient husband who watched me struggle
with this subject for a long time will never read this book,
but his sweet attitude is written on every page.

THANKS....

●　●　●　●

To all the relatives and friends who let me sit at their table or on their floor to do this work—Alice Little, Randy and Krystle Maddox, Barbara "Bright City" Kopp, and others, sometimes learning I worked through the night, then getting it sent out for me. Roger Ferris and Brian Strayer, who corrected my mistakes and taught me much. And thanks to all who said, "Well, hurry up! I can't wait to read it!"

TABLE OF CONTENTS

● ● ● ●

FOREWORD

• • • •

Is this right or is this wrong? We deal with that question every day. Throughout history cultures around the world look at the essence of right living in many different ways. Even within groups and religions, *right* and *wrong* take on various meanings.

But there are ten universal principles that can influence every person in this world if they are followed, and would save lives, prevent wars, and help peace reign everywhere. Those principles were written in stone thousands of years ago by the finger of God. They are to this day hidden in a cave somewhere in the Middle East.

They are housed in a golden chest, and though hidden, they influence the lives of the people mentioned in this book, the history of nations, and even your own personal life.

CHAPTER 1
EARTH'S DILEMMA— HOW IT ALL STARTED

● ● ● ●

Sometime before 4000 BC...

My name is Gabriel, and I am one of the angels closest to my Creator, Father God. He has appointed me to oversee the doings of angels in heaven and earth. So, I want to tell you the history of the great war between good and evil on your planet and what it has to do with that golden chest and the law inside—that chest that you people on earth have been trying to find for centuries. It all started in heaven. Let me tell you what happened:

With screaming and curses Satan and his angels left. Under the ultimatum of the Creator of the Universe they left. His tears revealed His broken heart, yet holy determination bathed His face. We angels watched with heavy hearts, too, as they exited heaven. With anger, hardness, and rebellion written on their faces, Lucifer (Satan) and his cohorts left the heights of heaven and were cast onto the newly created Earth. We angels could only imagine what trouble they were going to cause down there. We looked at each other, sighed, and shook our heads. We were sad, yet relieved.

Our Captain, Jesus, stood for a while looking into space; He had tried so hard to keep His family of angels together. After much pleading, reasoning, and warnings, their stubborn hatred had grown worse through the months, and there seemed but one thing to do: rid heaven of the evil that had sprouted and grown into a monstrous, choking vine, creeping along the ground, seizing and winding around anything within reach of its tendrils.

Lucifer and I had been best friends for many ages, ever since we were created by the gentle yet powerful words of God. We were given the job of being His closest servants, always by His side, constantly appreciating and loving Him for all the beautiful things He was doing. We were each given different talents for service, as were all the millions of our fellow angels that constantly came and went with special directions as the number of inhabited worlds expanded. My special spiritual gifts were compassion and strength. Lucifer's gifts were music and beauty. Both of us, working together under the wise direction of God, helped make heaven and the planets places of joy and love.

But then something happened. I can't explain it. Why Lucifer began to complain to me about some of the things God was doing was beyond me. I tried to explain the wisdom of God's decisions. But then he'd say, "If I were …" I tried to reason with him, but then things got worse. Our Captain, God's Son, who was Best Friend to both of us, also tried to explain things, and tried to reason with him, laboring for months on different issues that, it seemed to me, were nothing but worthless ambition coming from a created being arguing with his Creator.

> *My special spiritual gifts were compassion and strength. Lucifer's gifts were music and beauty. Both of us, working together under the wise direction of God, helped make heaven and the planets places of joy and love.*

Not only did it all take up a lot of precious time for our Captain, but Lucifer began talking among the other angels, grumbling that if he were the one running things everything would be different. "Why, if everybody is good, does there have to be a law? Why can't every angel follow his own plans instead of running errands all the time? If everyone is equal, why are God and His Son ordering everybody around? They are just being self-important. Why does there have to be such a thing as a government anyway?"

Goal-setting became Lucifer's mindset: "I'm going to be like the Most High. I'm going to do better when I get there," he told all who would listen.

Jesus, the Captain of the Host, continued to help and guide, but the time came when Lucifer declared war. He had recruited a third of the angels by convincing them that God the Father was not worthy of honor, that Jesus was an imposter, and that the throne could be taken. I honestly don't know why he thought he could win a war, but anyway, in the end, when God and all of us agreed that enough was enough, Lucifer and his angels were expelled to Earth. We were relieved.

But relief did not last for long. The arch rebel determined to take over Planet Earth, that place of exquisite beauty, every system in nature working perfectly for the smooth operation of life and continuous progress. If he thought he could keep all that going by himself, he was more insane than we thought.

But he was determined to turn Earth into his domain, and earthlings into servants of himself. He deceived the first man and woman, invading God's perfect creation. Their choice—touching and eating of the forbidden tree—marked and sealed the destiny of the human race. By inherited tendencies, the children of each generation deteriorated until the world of nature and the nature of man was scarred, discolored, maimed, and hopelessly rushing toward oblivion. Satan put within the heart of man hatred for the law of love and replaced it with his own love of self. But for the intercession of God and His Son, Earth was doomed.

Sometimes God the Father would say to me, "Gabriel, go down there and help those troubled souls." So, now and then I would appear to men, women, and children. I went down even to Jesus Himself on earth when He needed me. We angels always loved to help earthlings, especially those who were trying to do right. We received the ability to disguise ourselves and appear as humans in order to help. But Satan, and his angels, received the same ability to disguise themselves as people, even impersonating those who had died. They tried to deceive, steal, kill, and destroy everybody.

Satan said to his angel followers, "If I can make Jesus do something wrong while He's a human on earth, then I'll win the war. If I can destroy Him, then it will all be mine."

When Jesus died on the cross, Satan thought he had gained the victory. But on the third day, Jesus rose from the dead, and that resurrection sealed Satan's doom.

Christ promised He would return to Earth to rescue those who gave themselves to Him. The exact day or hour of His coming only God knows. But until He returns in the clouds, Satan and his angels work feverishly to destroy everything and everybody.

CHAPTER 2
THE REFUGEE

● ● ● ●

1517–1491 BC...

Somewhere in the Middle East a golden chest is hidden, its contents valued far above gold, rubies, and pearls. To learn about this priceless treasure, we must examine the life of one man, in particular, who is connected to the inception and early history of this hidden treasure. His name was Moses...

From the night shadows of the palace emerged the prince, his tall figure, bent in fear, moving quickly from gloom to darkness through the sleeping city and into the countryside. Once beyond range of notice, Moses broke into a run, taking a little used path. The desert wind blew sand in his face, but years of military training had prepared him for the rigors of travel, usually by Arabian horse, but now on foot.

As soon as word of his crime reached his grandfather, the king, the whole Egyptian army would be after him. How could he possibly escape? His heart pounded from exertion and from sadness at the thought of his action. How could he do such a thing? He had murdered one of God's creatures; it had been done in a moment of anger. Having discovered an Egyptian taskmaster beating one of the Hebrew slaves, he had struck the Egyptian, the slave had escaped, and the deed was done. This was the beginning of his campaign to free the slaves, his fellow Hebrews. He quickly buried the body in the sand before anyone saw him.

But someone had seen him. As he oversaw construction the next day, two Hebrews fought each other in anger, and he had commanded them to get back to work. "So are you going to kill me like you killed the Egyptian yesterday?" snapped one of them.

That was suddenly the end of his campaign; the lifelong goal of taking his people to the Promised Land had gone awry. Even his own blood hated him now. He walked away as calmly as possible, knowing he now had to disappear somehow. But where? Back in his room he quickly gathered a small pack of supplies that he could hide under his clothing. Again, his survival training paid off.

What would they do to his mother? The princess had loved him from the moment she discovered him, a three-month old, floating in a little basket in the reeds. She had adopted him immediately and had overseen his apprenticeship as the heir to the throne of the most powerful empire in the Mediterranean.

And what would they do to Jochebed, his biological mother? Would they question her? His heart ached for her, that humble little woman whose faith in the God of Heaven had seen to it that he learned the principles of true living. The princess had hired her to train the young child, probably knowing she was his own mother. One of those principles was not to kill.

At that thought his strength gave out and he collapsed in a heap. How could he go on? He had dishonored the God who had given him so much. How could he have betrayed his own people by thinking he could free them by violence? He wanted to say something to God, but how could he? And God probably wouldn't listen anyway. Finding a small scrub bush in the moonlight and wrapping himself in his mantle, he curled up and fell into an exhausted sleep.

Later, awaking suddenly, he jumped up, thinking someone was coming. What was it? Maybe a night creature. But now he readied himself to begin again. It was hard to see, but he could make out the small road by moonlight. He had followed the stars many miles southeast and was now farther away from the main travel routes that the Egyptians would certainly traverse in their search for him.

For several days and nights, he walked, his feet beginning to ache. But he knew he must trudge on. Now and then coming upon Bedouin encampments, he welcomed the sight of an occasional oasis, where he could fill his goatskin water bag and even soak his feet.

Soon, the terrain began to change from desert dunes to hills, then mountains. Finally, he greeted with quiet joy grass, small streams, green bushes, and an occasional stand of trees. A flock of sheep appeared, grazing in the fresh grass. He heard a human voice, and the shepherd's greeting sounded good to his lonely ears.

The mountains of Midian ... His mother had once told him she had a brother in Midian. But where? Midian was such a large place. And he was definitely lost—in more ways than one. That morning he stopped in surprise as he saw his first shepherdess. He would discover she was the first of many. At one watering hole, he saw several more shepherdesses. They cared for a large flock of sheep. They seemed to be arguing with some men. He watched. The discussion seemed to be about whose watering hole it was. The shepherds were trying to prove their dominance a little more than they should, but the girls stood their ground, until threats and shouts filled the peaceful valley.

The entire group of shepherds paused as the tall regal figure approached them.

"Why are you arguing? There's plenty of water for all these sheep!"

Finally, the commanding presence of Moses in his Egyptian garb cause the shepherds to retreat. The girls finished their watering and started for home. They returned, however, to thank the stranger for his intercession, and asked him, "Where are you from?" and "Where are you going?" ... questions he could answer only vaguely. But they liked his looks, his polite manner, his direct gaze, and his cultured way of speaking, so much so that they told their father when they got home.

Moses had settled in for the night in some trees near the pond when he looked up and saw the girls coming back.

"Our father has invited you to come home to eat with us and stay the night." The girls looked as if they were as happy about the idea as Moses felt in his heart.

When the two men met and talked, there seemed to be an invisible bond between them.

As the old man asked questions, Moses tried to evade them as he had with the girls. But Jethro (Reuel) looked closely into Moses' face and eyes and said, "You know, I have a sister living in Egypt. She used to have the job of raising an adopted son of the Princess. He's grown up now, and I understand he has become quite a successful general and is heir to the throne..." Jethro tilted his head slightly, his eyes steady on Moses' face.

It seemed to Moses that Jethro's eyes penetrated his soul. Moses caught his breath. *He knows!* His heart leaped.

Jethro continued, "Actually, you look quite a bit like..."

"Are you my mother's brother?... You are my uncle?" What a relief to Moses. This kind, wise man was his own family!

"Son, why are you here? Why are you so far from your home and your responsibilities?"

With understanding encouragement from Jethro, Moses told his story.

That night as Moses prepared to sleep in his uncle's home, he knew God had directed him to this safe place, had heard his prayer of repentance, had observed his tears, and had saved him. He knew now that God had not left him alone.

It seemed to Moses that Jethro's eyes penetrated his soul. Moses caught his breath. He knows! His heart leaped.

For forty years, Moses guarded Jethro's sheep. During that time, he wrote much. Under the influence of God's Holy Spirit, and from his knowledge of history, he wrote the Book of Genesis. He also married Zipporah, one of the seven shepherdesses, and had two sons.

One day while he wandered with his sheep to find fresh grazing, he saw a bush not far away that burned with an intense fire, but it strangely did not burn up. He approached it for a closer look, and when he did a voice came from heaven saying: "Take off your shoes from off your feet, for the place whereon thou standest is holy ground!"

From this spot, Moses learned that his life ambition to free his people from Egyptian slavery could still be accomplished—if he did it God's way and not his own.

So, from this beginning, Moses went back to the Pharaoh's court to intercede for the Israelites, and at first was refused. He followed God's directions to return time after time, through the months of the ten plagues that radically reduced Egypt's power and population. The Hebrew slaves, untouched by the plagues, finally reached their freedom by crossing the Red Sea on dry ground.

From the top of Mount Sinai Moses received Ten Commandments written by God's own finger, the rule of life for all mankind. He also received instructions for building an elegant portable sanctuary where God could live with His people. In this sanctuary were pieces of furniture, symbolic of the spiritual life, one of which was a golden chest.

CHAPTER 3

GOD'S SHOW AND TELL

● ● ● ●

1491 BC...

Three million hearts stood still. In breathless silence the freed slaves watched the cloud descend slowly. Little children pointed. After seven months of anxious hard work and giving, they watched. Would God accept their work—the newly-constructed tent temple He had commanded to be built so He could live with them? Now as the bright cloud floated downward toward the sanctuary the people trembled. Slowly. Slowly. And now it entered through the curtained doorway. Accepted!

The people could breathe easily again, but they didn't know whether they should silently pray their thanks or sing and shout. They did both.

The three men who led the construction stood together: Moses, who received the blueprints up on the nearby mountain; Bezaleel, the project manager; and Aholiab, his assistant. They looked at each other with triumphant smiles.

Moses put his hands on the shoulders of Bezaleel and Aholiab, "Thank you both so much for your efforts, especially for directing all the workers."

Let us listen to Bezaleel, the project manager, tell of his experience: "Imagine my surprise seven months ago, when Moses sent me word to come see him—this leader of millions—vigorous, clear-eyed, mentally and physically strong for his eighty years. What a privilege to sit before such a man! But why was I there, just a humble artisan, hardly known by anyone? There are a few who recognized me as the great grandson of Caleb, one of the twelve spies who had searched out the Promised Land and had come back with a good report.

The information I received puzzled me further. I had been appointed by the great sovereign God to work directly for Him! I stared in speechless surprise at the official call by Moses for me to become project manager of probably the most significant, symbolic structure ever built in history: the first abiding place for God on Earth!

Moses showed me the blueprints he had made during his stay on Mt Sinai, 7,500 feet above the desert floor. Oh, they were extensive, detailed in every dimension. The list of materials needed ... the directions ... all had been written by hand on top of that rugged mountain! Every detail was described—all except how it was to be accomplished. The method, the timing ... that was to be my job.

My brain began working. If the God of Heaven had called me to do it, then would He provide the wisdom to do it?

I marveled that while there were some Egyptians who had come across the Red Sea and traveled with us through the wilderness who were expert craftsmen, God had called *me*, experienced only in making bricks. He promised me wisdom, artistic and management abilities. He also appointed me a helper, Aholiab, a faithful Israelite.

Yes! If God told me to do something, then it was important that I do it, and do it well. Suddenly determination filled my heart and mind.

Yes! If God told me to do something, then it was important that I do it, and do it well. Suddenly determination filled my heart and mind. I set to work immediately, calling for materials: fine linen taken from Egypt, acacia wood from the river bank, animal skins, dyes from plants and shells, gold and silver, gems brought from Egypt. Oh! How exciting, how beautiful it was going to be! The people responded with overwhelming generosity. I had to organize it all: jewels, brass mirrors, looms, tools, skeins of fine linen. Volunteer craftsmen and women came, skilled in metalwork, weaving, gem cutting, embroidery, spinning of goats' hair, and seasoning skin of sea animals.

Each craft occupied its own territory with raw material, tools, and storage. Often in my job of organizing, I stood amazed at the innovation of the workers, their enthusiasm, and their willingness to follow directions to the letter.

My assistant, Aholiab, took part in the supervision and we both worked with our hands, according to plan. Moses himself would come around, pleased at the progress he observed, and give encouragement to all, and he received it in turn. Every day we saw advancement.

On Friday afternoons, we all straightened up our work place, cleaned and put away our tools, stored our materials and finished work, then cleaned ourselves up in time to meet the Lord's Sabbath at sundown. The seventh day was spent in worship, prayer, singing, eating, spending time with our families and friends, and getting badly needed rest from work, business, and the cares of the world. Pharaoh, back in Egypt, wouldn't let us rest for even one day and increased our labors when we asked for Sabbaths off until we thought we'd die. Some did.

At the end of seven months, under Moses' encouragement and direction, we finished building the tabernacle—God's dwelling place—with all its furniture and contents. The time for a great and solemn celebration ceremony arrived.

Let me tell you what happened. During our prayer of dedication, a great cloud came down, the same cloud that shielded us from the heat by day and from cold by night all during our journey to this mountain called Sinai. As the thousands of us stood and watched, awestruck, the cloud slowly entered our new structure and remained there! The presence of the Creator of heaven and Earth accepted with pleasure His new dwelling place with us, His children.

We rejoiced! Everyone's face shone with satisfaction and new hope. Even the women who gave their brass mirrors for construction material, looked better than ever before, their faces aglow with devotion and satisfaction!

Let me show you this dwelling place of our God.

Here you see a court surrounded by a fence of luxurious linen. This was made using 250 fine threads woven together in each inch, yet it is transparent. The Egyptians liked to clothe their women in dresses made of linen so fine it could be drawn through a finger ring. This linen was given to us by our slave masters as we left Egypt. I believe God impressed them to do that—otherwise they never would have parted with such elegant fabric.

Here inside the court sits a large altar. A repentant sinner comes in with a sheep, puts his hand on its head and confesses his wrong, then with a sharp knife, cuts its throat. The sheep dies quietly and slowly. There are a lot of mixed feelings for a person to watch an innocent animal die in his place, but the principle is there. Then a priest takes some of the sheep's blood in a bowl. It is then burned on the altar. The sheep takes the place of the sinner and pays for his guilt, and at the same time symbolizes the Messiah to come, who will sacrifice Himself for the sins of all who sincerely repent.

And here is the laver with water for the washing of the priest's hands and feet, preparing him to enter the tabernacle. The sides of the sanctuary are boards of acacia (a rot-and-insect-proof wood we got from the riverside) covered with pure gold. The roof of the tabernacle is covered with several layers. The top is woven goat hair and skins of the dugong, a river animal. The under layer is fine linen embroidered with colored and silver strands that sparkle in the lamplight.

Here to the left stands this large lampstand of solid gold with seven lights reflecting on the golden walls and ceiling veil. It burns constantly and is fed by wicks in pure beaten olive oil. It symbolizes the Son of God who will come and be called the Light of the World.

Here to your right stands this table holding two plates of flat loaves of unleavened bread. This symbolizes the Word of God, the Holy Scriptures, and also the Word who is the Messiah to come, the Creator of the World—the Bread of Life.

Here in front of this beautiful curtain of fine linen, embroidered again with colorful flowers, fruit, leaves, and angels, stands the smaller altar of incense upon which the blood is sprinkled. The smoke of the burning frankincense and myrrh rises in colored sparkles to the top of this curtain and into the next room. This depicts the prayers of the people and of the Son of God.

Now, here in the next room, the most holy place, on the inner side of the beautiful curtain, stands a large golden chest called the ark of the covenant. It's more than four feet long and about two-and-a-half feet high and wide. Inside are two tables of stone upon which is written the Ten Commandments written by the finger of God. The cover, called the mercy seat, is of solid gold with golden, lacy filigree around the edge. And here you see atop the cover two golden angels facing downward toward the cover of the chest, with one of their wings touching that of the other, and the other wing wrapped around themselves. Between the angels is the Presence of God. He has chosen this tiny speck of earth in which to live because His people have had to struggle against Satan's deceptions for so many years. He wants to live with His beloved people and give them hope and a happy, productive life.

This is but a concise picture of the detailed and beautiful place where ceremonies are held that express our love to God and His love for us. He has provided a system for us to be free of guilt of past sins. This sanctuary and its ceremonies symbolize the life, death, and resurrection of God's Son, who will someday come and give His life instead of a sacrificed lamb. He will be called The Lamb of God.

CHAPTER 4
DESTINY IN PROGRESS

● ● ● ●

About 1405 BC...

Anger etched his face, fire blazed from his eyes, his hands clutched the rod with such intensity that his knuckles turned white. With a shout and a fierce swing of the heavy stick, the rock responded to the blow by pouring forth drinking water. By this fit of temper, the perfect, earthly career of God's best friend came to an end.

Still as strong physically as a young man, this servant leader, Moses, had enthusiastically received almost 100 years of strict schooling, military training, and preparation for royalty in the largest and strongest empire in the western world. He remained faithful and loved by his adopted Egyptian family, by his beloved troops, by his cavalry and Egyptian horses, but he could no longer remain true to both Egypt and his Israelite heritage. Though he remained true and devoted to his blood family, the time came when he had to leave it all, and launch into a completely different identity, a new life far away. This 100 years included forty years as a shepherd, an author, a husband and father, and another forty years as servant leader to millions of freed and ignorant slaves, trying to train them to become stable, loyal citizens of God's kingdom.

From mental fatigue and continual stress, his mind had failed. All the orderly cells and elements of his brain scattered, as it were, and he collapsed at the feet of his Best Friend. But that Best Friend did not abandon him, nor all the people he had led through the years. But they must have a leader that maintained humble equilibrium.

Joshua, the closest and most faithful human friend of Moses, watched as the 120-year-old man prepared to climb the mountain for the last time. He stood amazed as he arranged his few possessions in orderly fashion for someone else to take after his departure. What energy! Yet, a sadness permeated the atmosphere unexpressed until now. Joshua knew Moses had worked diligently under terrible and discouraging circumstances for forty years traveling through the wilderness of the Sinai Peninsula, camping at no less than twenty-nine locations. The people had complained constantly, criticizing all his decisions that had come down from God Himself. Moses had remained faithful through it all—until two days ago.

He had taken upon himself the credit instead of honoring God for supplying water from the rock. Later, before the God whom he loved, Moses repented and conceded that possibly he no longer had the stamina to lead the people. But to miss going into the Promised Land after all those years? It was a bitter disappointment.

Up the 7,500-foot mountain he had climbed, not as an old man, but with the vigor of a young man. He had good eyesight yet, and he looked like a thirty-year-old ascending the rugged, boulder-strewn height. As Moses disappeared into the high-altitude mist, Joshua turned around to face his new charge. This was not the same excited crowd that had crossed the Red Sea, but their children. All the complaining, angry, whimpering ones had died in the wilderness. Only he, Moses, and Caleb had survived the forty-year trek. Now it would be up to him and Caleb to lead the people across the Jordan into the land they had inherited. God would be their Guide and Provider.

Joshua remembered forty years ago when he and Caleb, along with ten other spies, had crossed the Jordan by night and entered the promised country, avoiding, by all means, the inhabitants. They had toured the countryside after the farmers had finished their work in the fields and gone back into their walled cities and shut the gates. What the spies found, as they traveled by night, startled their hungry senses. The fragrance of fresh fruit on the trees, the taste of oranges and grapes, the flowers blossoming all around, the ripened grain, turned their discouraged hearts toward this place as nothing else could. However, from their hiding places during the day, they watched strong, hardy workmen laboring in the harvest fields. Tall, muscular porters balanced huge baskets of grain and fruit on their shoulders or carried them to wagons to be hauled to town. Uniformed soldiers, great in form and stature, guarded the cities. During the almost six weeks the spies searched out the land, they counseled with one another to assess their situation. Most doubted they could take the cities. They watched the huge men going about their work. There was no way these people could be conquered! But the fragrance of the fruit, the trees, the flowers, the beauty of the hills and forests, spoke to their homesick hearts after spending their lives in a hot, sandy desert.

Joshua and Caleb had agreed, but their approach to the problem was different, "Let us go up at once, and possess it; for we are well able to overcome it." But when the other spies had complained, Joshua had encouraged them. "The land which we passed through to search it, is an exceeding good land. If the Lord delights in us, then he will bring us into this land and give it us, a land which flows with milk and honey. Only rebel not against the Lord, neither fear the people of the land, for they are bread for us; their defense is departed from them, and the Lord is with us; fear them not." But nothing could change the minds of the remaining ten spies.

So they had returned to the river, and silently paddled their raft to the other side. Their families rushed to the shore to greet them. Moses, also, anxious for their return, had greeted them with smiles and hugs.

But the joy lasted only a short time, "There are giants there! We can't do it," cried the ten spies.

"Yes, we can!" retorted Joshua and Caleb, "The Lord has seen us through the Red Sea; He has given us water and food. He has promised!"

But the negatives had permeated the camp. Millions of "we can't do it" words were spoken during that night, which made almost everyone grumpy as they got up the next morning.

Moses knelt before God, saying, "What can I do, Lord?" And God answered, "If they don't trust Me after all I've done for them, what else can I do? Tell the people that for every day the spies spent in the land I have promised you, that number of years it will take you to get there! Your disbelief, complaining, and rebellion will come down on your own heads."

And so that's the way it was for forty years. All the people who had crossed the Red Sea and who had seen the power of God, continued to complain, blame, moan, and cause trouble, until not one of them was left. The sands of the Sinai Peninsula contain the bodies of two million precious people. Their shoes had not worn out, but they themselves had perished in the wilderness. Their children, who had crossed the Red Sea on their parents' backs, had inherited their shoes and somehow had learned to trust God, listen to His words, and do right—knowing this was the best way to survive hardship. Out of the multitude who had crossed the Red Sea forty years ago, only two of the original adults crossed the Jordan. These now grown-up children were finally ready to follow Joshua and Caleb across the river to the Promised Land.

> *Out of the multitude who had crossed the Red Sea forty years ago, only two of the original adults crossed the Jordan. These now grown-up children were finally ready to follow Joshua and Caleb across the river to the Promised Land.*

Plans to leave progressed. There were some special treasures that needed to go with them. Along with the company that crossed the Jordan was to be carried the embalmed body of Joseph, the Israelite prime minister of Egypt, who, almost a hundred years before, had requested that he might be privileged to enter the Promised Land with the people of God. His sarcophagus had accompanied the materials for the sanctuary and the tools of trade brought from Egypt across the Red Sea, and now across the Jordan.

Also, along with them was to go "Aaron's rod that budded," which came from the experience in the wilderness when some had complained that Moses and his brother, Aaron, were not qualified to lead the people and a rebellion had ensued. Finally, to quell the rebellion, God told Moses to have the leader of each of the twelve tribes bring a stick with his tribe's name inscribed on it. All the rods were put before the ark and left overnight. The next morning the rod of Aaron and Moses had brought forth leaves, blossoms— and fully matured almonds! So the leadership of Moses and Aaron was established.

Along with the ark, and the rod that budded, a "pot of manna" was to be included. This container held a sample of the food that had fallen morning by morning to feed the millions of people camping and traveling. They were to gather a certain amount every day for each individual, no less and no more. If they gathered more than they needed, it would spoil. On the sixth day only, were they to gather enough for the next day, the Sabbath, and it did not spoil. On Sabbath morning there was no manna on the ground. And if anyone had neglected to gather enough on Friday, they were disappointed—and hungry. The morning of the first day of the week, the manna fell again and on through the week. What a miracle! For forty years it had continued.

And now, suddenly the shout was heard, "It's time to go!" The sanctuary was disassembled, folded, wrapped, and readied for the trip across the Jordan. Families packed their possessions and their tents; the camp area was cleaned and would be left without a trace of careless neglect. The families assembled according to their tribes and waited for the word from God to advance. At the head of the company, borne by the tribe of Levi, moved the ark, the mysterious Golden Chest. The wings of the golden angels atop the ark pointed to heaven from under its blue cover, as if giving praise to God for His eternal patience and hope in His earthly children. Excitement filled the morning air.

"Go forward! God is with us!"

Filing into perfect order according to their tribe, their banners held high, the procession began. As the priests, carrying the ark by its staves on their shoulders, approached the river's edge, their hearts beat faster and their feet hesitated. The great mass of people began to sing their anthem of praise to God. With shouts and cheers, the parents lifted their burdens and babies. The priests descended the river bank and stepped into the water. Suddenly the water stopped flowing, and water piled high to the side as if by an invisible dam. Even the mud underneath turned to solid ground. Nothing could slow the feet of men, women, children, cattle, sheep, and goats; thousands of feet crossed over on dry ground. What a miracle! No army pursuing this time, the land of milk and honey, promise and opportunity, lay ahead. The crossing of the Jordan proved to be one of the greatest events in the history of the world. And the ark led the way!

CHAPTER 5

A COAL SNATCHED
FROM THE BURNING

● ● ● ●

1451 BC...

Voices and loud banging on the door brought the innkeeper, dressed in her nightclothes with a lamp in her hand, quickly to open the door to military police who pushed and crowded in, almost knocking her down.

"Where are they?" the police demanded, "The king has sent word to you saying, 'Bring forth the men that are come to you, which are entered into your house: for they come to search out all the country.'"

As they hurried from room to room, Rahab replied, "There came men unto me, but I don't know where they came from, and it happened about the time of shutting of the gate, when it was dark, that they went out. Where they went I don't know. Pursue after them quickly for you shall overtake them."

As soon as they had left, she bolted the door, and hurried quickly and silently up the stairs to the roof where she had hidden the two spies. They had knocked quietly at her door earlier in the night. She was used to those quiet knocks. Men came often for her services, so she was surprised that these two strangers wanted only sleeping space and a little food. Their clean looking faces and different style of clothing told her they must be Israelites. Their straightforward manner and clear eyes told her these were not the idolatrous men of her city who participated in the degrading rituals that she had begun to question long ago. Her profession gave her the money she needed and even from that she hoped she could somehow escape. Unlike the idols her people worshipped, she had heard that the Israelite's God was alive and powerful. She wanted to know more. She had led these two men upstairs to the roof, knowing they would be hunted down, and hid them under sheaves of drying flax. The police had searched her place, even the roof, but did not discover the hidden pair.

Now it was time to quickly review the agreement she had made with them before they lay down under the sheaves of flax on the roof. She had said to them, "I know that the Lord has given you the land, and we all are terrified, and everybody in this place faints because of you. We've known for many years how the Lord dried up the water of the Red Sea for you, when you came out of Egypt, and how you have destroyed the kingdoms on the other side of Jordan. As soon as we had heard these things, our hearts melted, and we've all become completely discouraged because of you, for the Lord your God, He is God in heaven above, and in earth beneath. So now, I pray you, swear to me by the Lord, since I have showed you kindness, that you will also show kindness to my father's house, and give me a true token, that you will save the lives of my father, and my mother, and my brothers and my sisters, and all that they have, and save us!"

And the men answered her, "Our life for yours; if you utter not this our business, the Lord will deal kindly and truly with you."

Now as she prepared the rope to let them down out of her window facing the fields outside the city, she warned, "Get you to the mountain, lest the pursuers meet you; and hide yourselves there three days, 'til they come back; and after that, go your way."

And the men replied, "We will be blameless of your oath which you made us swear. So when we come into the land, you shall bind the line of scarlet in the window which you let us down by; and then bring your father and all your family into your house with you. Whoever shall go out of the doors of your house into the street, his blood shall be upon his head, and we will be guiltless, and whoever shall be with you in the house, his blood shall be on our head, if any are hurt. And if you utter this our business, then we will be free of our oath to you"

And she said, "According unto your words, so be it."

So Rahab let the men down out of her window by a rope. Then she secured the rope that would hang from her window in the city wall. When the spies were not found by the king's men who had gone to the ford in the Jordan, the citizens found a bit of relief, but not enough to comfort them. The harvest was mostly finished, so keeping the gates closed during the day helped them feel better. The thick walls with homes inside of them had protected the city for many years. With the harvested grain inside the city, they could survive a long time.

On the fourth day after the spies disappeared, reports came from those on watch that the Israelites were gathering at the other side of the river. The Jordan, swollen by the spring runoff, suddenly stopped its flow, water piling up on the upper side. First came four priests in their white robes carrying the golden chest with its angels covered with a blue cover. Thousands crossed over on dry ground.

They found her and her family crying in terror, and pulling them out through the rubble, led them away from the blazing city into the field toward the river.

After another three days, the same procession approached Jericho—first the trumpeters, then the ark, then all the priests, and then the soldiers and people. Silently they marched around the city, then went back to their camp. The next day they came back, marched around again once, then back home. For six days this happened. Rahab kept her family in her house inside the wall, warning them to not leave.

But on the seventh day, the procession circled the city seven times and then stopped. Suddenly from the line, the sound of loud ram's horn trumpets rent the air, the people shouted, and with a terrifying crash, Jericho's walls began to crumble from the inside out. The Israelites rushed in, destroying every living thing and burning all of Jericho's towers and palaces.

Meanwhile, the two spies rushed into Rahab's home, the only spot in the wall still intact. They found her and her family crying in terror, and pulling them out through the rubble, led them away from the blazing city into the field toward the river.

That evening, when the army returned home, they took with them Rahab, her parents, and her family. Israelite families welcomed them all into their tent-homes, giving them comfort in the midst of their intensely mixed emotions of grief and gratitude.

The ark of the covenant, the symbol of God's presence, with the Commandments inside, gave protection and success to His people when they obeyed Him. It still does.

Rahab, who had desired a better, cleaner life, now worshipped the true God, becoming a devoted believer. Later she married an Israelite, Salmon, and eventually became known to us today as the great-great grandmother of King David and an ancestor of the Lord Jesus Christ.

CHAPTER 6

THE GOLDEN MICE

● ● ● ●

About 1100 BC...

Shrieks of terror and shouts of anger inside the vast idol temple rent the quiet early morning air in Ashdod, Philistia; several priests burst from the massive door and ran down the staircase into the city below, their robes flying in the confusion.

"He's done it again! This time, it's done! It's over!"

A sleepy-eyed crowd gathered in wonder as the priests explained in shouts, their arms waving, and fists raised high.

"He's done it again! This time he's destroyed our god! He cut off his head! And his arms! Our fish-man fell down in front of the golden chest as if worshipping it. That golden chest must be the Israelites' god! He is powerful!"

Three mornings before, a celebration parade had entered Ashdod with weary yet exultant troops, carrying what they believed to be the god of the Israelites, the ark of the covenant. Its blue covering still in place, the warriors had not dared to remove it. The Philistines, long-standing enemies of God's people in the Promised Land, had listened to their soothsayers and false prophets, believing they could conquer the hated Israelites. But as long as God's people chose to love and show loyalty to Him, He prospered them in gaining pagan land. But Israel had failed.

The Philistine captain had joined his troops in preparing to return home from the battle, "And we've got their god to prove our victory!" At the rear of the company, the sacred ark was conveyed into the city to the temple of their god, Dagon. Great celebrations followed.

The next day a young Philistine priest had assumed new responsibilities: a new god in the temple of his fish-god, Dagon, called the "Protector of the Sea." That great image, with its upper part resembling a man, and the lower part a fish, had been placed in this magnificent temple long ago. As he walked through the city to work, the priest pondered the thousands of Philistine and Israelite warriors who lay dead on the battlefield beyond, waiting to be burned or buried or taken up in the dark of night by mourning relatives.

The priest's thoughts turned to that chest with the blue cover. *Isn't it supposed to protect the Israelites in their wars and give them victories? Why did they lose? I've heard that some of them worship all kinds of other gods and images that are worse than the worst. Could that be the cause of their misfortunes?*

He had climbed the stairs of the temple that contained the god, Dagon. This image stood opposite the ark of the covenant, which was covered with a blue mantle. But, as he opened the massive doors, he gasped in horror. There on the floor before the ark lay Dagon, face down, as if worshipping the chest. Cries of help that day brought other priests and the village men who placed Dagon again to his place of honor and returned to their day's work.

But now, the next morning, the priests had discovered Dagon not only on the floor, but with his head and arms broken off as if someone had sawed them off above the elbows. No question now! The God of the Israelites was expressing His anger. Now what to do?

Then other things started happening. The Philistine men began getting sick; their private parts began to bleed—the parts that had much to do with the worship of their fish-man god, Dagon. Many died from this painful plague, causing families to mourn, and raising questions among the priesthood.

Thinking that moving the ark to another city might solve the problem, the people of Ashdod sent it to Gath, but the same thing happened there—more death. So, on it went to the next city, Ekron, where the people cried, "What are you doing to us? Are you trying to kill us?"

For seven long months the people of Philistia suffered the anger of the Israelites' God. The Philistines then decided to take the ark out into the country; but then mice came by the thousands, into the grain fields, the houses, the food bins, and even into people's beds!

The pagan priests of the Philistines finally gathered together to seek a solution. Remembering the oral and written history of five hundred years before when God had sent plagues down upon Egypt because they had enslaved the Israelites, some of their older wisc men suggested they return the fearful symbol of the presence of their God to the Israelites.

But how to do that? Some of the priests suggested they send it by a cart drawn by two mother cows separated from their babies: if the mothers headed toward the nearest Israelite community without anyone guiding them, then they would know that Israel's God had done this.

They made and offered sacrifices to their gods for healing. Five golden replicas of the male organs that were affected in the Philistine men, along with five golden mice, representing each of the lordships of Philistia, were fashioned, and placed in a coffer beside the ark on a brand-new cart, drawn by two nursing oxen.

It worked. The two oxen, lowing for their babies as they went, pulled the cart holding the golden chest with its two golden angels, still covered with its bright blue covering, representing truth, toward a field being worked near Bethshemesh in Israel. The field workers looked up in surprise, and shouted, "Here comes our ark!"

But the celebration that followed caused even worse trouble than before! After they had made a fire, burning the cart and the oxen as a thank offering, they became curious. The people had come in from the far corners of the region to see the ark, but they wanted to SEE it, so they tore off the sacred shroud, something the Philistines dared not do, seized the solid gold cover with the attached golden angels, and set it on the ground—the mercy seat of the Presence of their Creator on the ground! Then they looked inside the sacred golden chest. There lay the Ten Commandments written on tables of stone. Thousands passed by looking in. And thousands died—more than 50,000 of them!

What a tragedy!

CHAPTER 7

UZZAH

● ● ● ●

1042 BC...

King David sat in his private quarters with his elbows on his knees, his head down. He couldn't get the scene out of his mind: the huge procession with the ark on a cart pulled by two oxen approaching a threshing floor. The oxen stumbled. A young man, Uzzah, walking alongside reached out to steady the ark and was killed instantly as if by a bolt of lightning. David's voice quavered as he spoke, "How could such a terrible thing happen?" He looked up at his old friend, Nathan the prophet, who sat opposite him.

It was the middle of the night. One candle burned, showing each man the troubled face of the other. It had been a bad day. No doubt, there were similar scenes in many homes that night. A tragedy beyond imagination had happened.

David shook his head, "I thought it was going to be a great, joyous occasion. More than thirty thousand people, priests, music with all sorts of instruments, choirs, the ark being carried to an honored place..."

Nathan stood up and peered out the palace window. Light in other homes burned also. "All I can say is, we didn't do it right. It's true that the ark has been in Adonijah's home for twenty years since the tragedy at Bethshemesh. Uzzah and his brother grew up with it in their home. I'm sure their parents warned them to stay away from it." He turned to face David, "It was admirable of you to want to take it to an honorable place here in your city until it could be put in the new temple. The idea of a big celebration was good also. But we didn't do it right."

"What do you mean?" David asked.

"According to the writings of Moses, the Lord specified how the ark should be transported. It is to be carried by poles inserted on each side and carried by priests on their shoulders."

"But didn't the Philistines send it back to Israel on a cart pulled by two oxen?" replied David. "And nothing happened then."

"But when the Philistines brought it back to Israel, what happened?" asked Nathan.

"The Israelite people took it all apart, looked inside, and they all died," answered David.

───── ● ● ● ─────

Yes, but we didn't do it right. God has instructed His people and we are to obey. To do things our way, tells Him we think we know best, and we don't know best.

───── ● ● ● ─────

Nathan said, "The Philistines didn't know. But the Israelites knew."

"The Lord is fair to the ignorant," said David.

"And we know. God gave us instructions a long time ago. And when the cart we made to transport the ark into the city shook because the oxen stumbled, Uzzah, walking next to it, became angry, took hold of the ark to steady it, and the Lord struck him down. The ark is the symbol of God's presence. No one except the priests can touch it." Nathan looked back out the window, "When will we learn not to treat such a holy thing like a piece of trash?"

David got up and stood beside his friend and watched the eastern sky begin to light up, "But I didn't treat it badly ... I was honoring it."

"Yes, but we didn't do it right. God has instructed His people and we are to obey. To do things our way, tells Him we think we know best, and we don't know best. Uzzah's death proves that."

The sun appeared over the horizon. David folded his hands and put them to his forehead, "Nathan, pray for me."

Nathan put his arm around David's shoulder, "Holy Father, You know we humans make so many mistakes. You call us to do things and we spoil everything by doing it our own way instead of Yours. You are so patient. It should have been us who died instead of Uzzah, but You have saved us to lead Your people in the right way. Please accept David's repentance, and mine, and we promise to do things right if You will stay with us. Amen."

And they did do it right. Three months later, another big procession went to Obed-Edom's house where the ark had been kept since the death of Uzzah. Obed-Edom and his family had been blessed in those three months.

The priests lifted the ark by its staves to their shoulders, and the large company, thirty thousand solders, players of stringed instruments, trumpets, tambourines, cymbals, and singers made their way into the city, making sacrifices every six steps to the God of Heaven and finally, the ark was settled in its new, temporary place to await its home in Solomon's temple.

CHAPTER 8
THE VISIT

● ● ● ●

992 BC...

Near the front of a swift Arabian dromedary caravan traveling along the acacia-lined Red Sea, a gilded covered seat, or "howdah," atop one of the animals swayed from side to side. Behind the protective curtain sat a queen. Her thoughts centered on what lie ahead. She thought, *After weeks of preparation and this long, long trip, will my efforts be worth it? Will my host appreciate my presence? Will he take the time to answer my questions? Will he treat my drivers and servants decently? What is the secret to his great fame?*

In the distance lay the great walled city of Jerusalem. The road was difficult to travel, with boulders on each side, narrowing occasionally into robber-infested passageways. Once she had seen through an opening in her curtain a runner greet her head driver, the runner then turning and running toward the city. Now her arrival would be known. Traveling around the deep ravine surrounding Jerusalem on the west, the caravan approached the city gate on the north. Her eyes widened as the gate opened and the king, with his retinue, emerged. Solomon rode upon a white Egyptian horse, his servants dressed in sun-repellant white.

Trumpets sounded, and a chorus sang as the king on his bejeweled horse descended to meet her. As the two companies met and stopped, the king dismounted, approached her howdah, and bowed. Her head driver placed a platform for her to descend, and as she reached the ground, the king reached out his hand and took hers. Greetings and conversation followed as he ushered her to a jeweled chair. As she took her place, four servants lifted the chair by two inserted poles. The king remounted his steed and led the caravan toward the city gate.

As they entered the gate, crowds greeted the queen with flowers and expressions of welcome. Many kings and rulers had visited King Solomon, but never such a beautiful queen. In spite of her weariness after months of travel, her heart beat faster, and tears came at this great moment in her life.

Gracious palace stewards guided her travel-weary drivers and servants to their quarters to clean up and rest. Shelter, provender, and grooming were supplied for her animals. The king, himself, showed the Queen of Sheba to her suite, her maids nearby, ready to help when needed. He didn't act like a pompous king at all, but like a humble, yet open and friendly servant. Was this why he was so loved by his people?

The next day, clean, refreshed and clothed in her morning garb of full cut trousers gathered at the ankles and jacket blouse, she met him at the appointed time to tour the palace grounds and city. The citizens seemed happy and reasonably prosperous; flowers grew in the windows and small yards. The narrow, hilly streets, clean and lined with townspeople, merchants, and children seemed to reflect the sunny disposition of the king as he greeted everyone and explained points of interest to her.

That evening, wearing her formal veil and jeweled gown, she attended a state dinner as the guest of honor. The king showed her the utmost kindness and respect. Attending also were important men of the city and their wives, military generals, and officers. She learned that her servants also were being honored elsewhere in the city by their peers.

During the next few months, the Queen was learning more and more from everyone surrounding her, while the king went about his work. Occasionally she met with him formally and informally. He taught her much through tours to the magnificent temple he had built to his God. Carved and gold lined, the high walls and ceilings glittered from the sun shining through the windows; elaborately embroidered curtains hung in the tall doorways; golden chains were draped artfully from place to place. The court contained the altar of sacrifice and the laver, as in the original sanctuary, built hundreds of years before in the wilderness of Sinai, but much greater in size and ornamentation. Twelve golden lions held the huge golden laver, each facing outward.

"What is the laver for?" she asked.

The king answered, "The priest must wash his hands and feet before entering the holy place."

The altar of brass stood in the large, elegant court. "What is this?" she asked.

"The priest sacrifices an animal and it is burnt as an offering to our Creator. This animal symbolizes God's Son to come who will be sacrificed to save humanity."

Neither she nor the king were allowed inside the holy sanctuary, so he explained the furniture, including the golden ark and the tables of stone inside

He showed her the ancient sanctuary built by Moses and Bezaleel with all their helpers newly freed from Egypt some six hundred years before, with its golden furniture still intact after its wanderings and adventures. It had been erected and stood proud in its special home within the great temple built by Solomon.

Her head and heart full of questions, the Queen asked, "When will God's Son come?" And her patient host explained all to her. The answers expanded her mind farther than she had ever experienced in her life.

She was allowed to examine the writings of Solomon's father, King David. He also allowed her to read what he himself had written.

"What are the Ten Rules written in stone?" she asked.

He named them all. Each of them proved reasonable and represented the right and wrong she had always known and felt.

She looked down, "But where do I stand? I've certainly broken most of them. How will I ever survive?"

Solomon gently put his finger under her chin and looked into her troubled face, "Take comfort, my dear lady. Though you don't belong to God's chosen people, you will find grace. He loves you, and He's willing to forgive and save all tender-hearted repentant ones. He will welcome you into His kingdom with open arms. The life blood shed by His Son when He comes will symbolize that forgiveness."

After showering gifts of gold, spices, and gems on the king through the months of her visit, and after receiving even more from him, the Queen of Sheba and her servants began the long trek home. As her howdah swayed from side to side, her mind whirled with happy thoughts and plans. She returned home not only satisfied, but dramatically changed.

She recorded her parting testimony to King Solomon as follows: "It was a true report that I heard in my own land of thy acts and of thy wisdom. Howbeit I believed not the words, until I came, and mine eyes had seen it; and, behold, the half was not told me; thy wisdom and prosperity exceedeth the fame which I heard. Happy are thy men, happy are these, thy servants, which stand continually before thee, and that hear thy wisdom. Blessed be the Lord thy God, which delighted in thee, to set thee on the throne of Israel; because the Lord loved Israel forever, therefore made he thee king, to do judgment and justice."

CHAPTER 9

ADVICE REJECTED

● ● ● ●

587 BC...

The loathsome muck at the bottom of the dungeon chilled the old man, as he landed, having been roughly lowered by ropes. He struggled to his feet and felt the mud cover his entire body, face and all. As he tried to stand upright, the foul mire came up to his neck. A chill ran up his spine and through his entire body. His enemies need not bother to kill him; they would need only leave him there until he collapsed from fatigue and drowned in the muck.

He struggled to move his legs in the thickness and dark. His hands touched cold stones. He leaned around the edge to determine the size of his new home. His faith in God had been tested—he had not failed his calling; but now King Zedekiah had allowed his counselors to do what they wanted with the old prophet, and they had banished him to ... this!

"We will not surrender!" They had shouted their refusal to surrender to God's proclamation that the citizens of Jerusalem must surrender to the Babylonians because of their many disloyalties toward Him. Jeremiah could say all that God instructed, but they were determined to fight to the end. He had repeatedly warned that if they kept up this idolatry, continued their vile practices, sacrificing their children in the fire, they would be destroyed. But the response of the leaders was always that since God had chosen them as His children, and had given them Jerusalem and the temple, they were guaranteed safety.

Meanwhile, the Chaldean army, strong and hungry for gold and blood, camped outside the walls of Jerusalem, building their war mounds to the height of the city walls, waiting ... waiting.

Inside the court, an Ethiopian servant, Ebedmelech, moved through the palace with an even more regal manner than his young master, Zedekiah, king of Judah. His gaze took in everything from the shine of the marble floors to the rich hangings on the wall, built with utmost care by King Solomon more than four centuries earlier. Other servants moved about their work. Deep in thought, Ebedmelech headed for the servants' quarters. Although a slave and a eunuch, he had made many friends. He liked these people and felt thankful he could work among believers in the God of Heaven. He himself believed and had loved to hear the stories from Jewish history, especially that of the Queen of Sheba, from southern Arabia, coming from near his home, a far distance from this city to visit King Solomon. His thoughts returned to his home, where the tribal religion and fear permeated the practices of everyone with no tolerance for other beliefs. But Ebedmelech felt confident that God had led him to the truth of Himself, the Creator of heaven and earth.

But now the Chaldeans had surrounded the city and were shooting their war darts over the wall into the city. The death rate was mounting.

The food was almost gone, the pestilence was spreading. Although the people were trying to keep up their courage by building similar war engines to fight back, the chances were slim.

Jeremiah had received word from the Lord that the people must go into captivity for seventy years because of their rejection of Him and because of their idolatry and its filthy practices. If they surrendered to Nebuchadnezzar they would live in safety. If not, their city would be leveled to the ground. But the princes refused to obey and talked the king into rejecting the message. The king, too weak in character to stand for the right, gave his counselors permission to do what they wished with Jeremiah. So God's servant was about to perish down here with mire up to his neck.

The king, upon hearing of Jeremiah's dangerous position, quickly gave Ebedmelech permission to rescue the prophet. Yes, Jeremiah is down there—in a big hole in the court so deep that anyone thrown down there had no way out. Gathering his equipment and thirty of his believing fellow workers together, he explained the situation, "Zedekiah is scared of his own shadow. He knows what he's done is wrong. He has given permission to pull Jeremiah out of the pit but wants everyone to keep quiet about it. He's the kind of man who doesn't want to do wrong, yet he's too weak to do what's right."

Later, in the court with the helpers standing by, Ebedmelech knelt at the edge of the dungeon and called down to the old man. A weak voice responded.

"We're going to let down a rope and some old clothes. Put them around your middle under your arms, and tie the rope around. Then we can pull you out without hurting you," Ebedmelech shouted.

"Oh, thank you! Bless you!" Jeremiah responded with new energy in his voice.

It took a while for the men to help Jeremiah reach the top and climb out onto firm pavement. He was covered in filth from head to toe.

Ebedmelech personally took charge of getting the exhausted prophet clean, warm, fed, rested, and comfortable, in spite of the tragic conditions existing throughout the palace.

Jeremiah expressed his thanks, "Oh, thank you, my true friend! I would have died down there"

Ebedemelech said, "My father, I want you to take new courage now. Never, never give up. Fulfilling the commission God has called you to do is the best way in the world you can honor your Maker and your people."

Later in the night Jeremiah heard a sound. Silently stealing toward Jeremiah's quarters came the young king. No one knew he had come. The old prophet sighed. Although still in reasonable health at his age, Jeremiah's work as a prophet and his repeated imprisonment had aged him considerably—but his work was not finished. Here came the regent of Judah.

In spite of his rich clothing, the king of Judah looked miserable. Worry etched his tanned face. Loose living and the shameful practices of idolatry had changed him and now fear was written across his face. "My kingdom is in danger; the Chaldeans are enlarging their encampment out there."

Again, Jeremiah repeated what he'd said time and time again, "My son, listen to me. You are not going to win! No matter what all your so-called advisors, your counselors, and important men say..." He watched as King Zedekiah stiffened. "This is God's message to you. You and our nation have gone too far. It is God's plan that you go into captivity to the Babylonians because you refuse to learn. Giving yourself, your time, your resources to your idols, sacrificing your own children to them, lowering yourselves in debauchery and detestable ceremonies, worshiping the sun ... what do you think God is anyway?... He is your loving Father—you are his children! How can you dishonor Him like this?"

The king stood to his feet, "Well, I can see you're still your old stubborn self in spite of your punishment."

> *"My father, I want you to take new courage now. Never, never give up. Fulfilling the commission God has called you to do is the best way in the world you can honor your Maker and your people."*

Jeremiah struggled to stand, "How can I tell you something that's not true? You are the chosen king of God's people. You are about to lose your country, your throne, your life if you don't surrender and do what you're told! If you open your eyes and your ears, you would learn what God has said: even if every Chaldean soldier either disappeared or died out there, and there were only two of them left and they were wounded, they would still take the city and burn it to the ground! No one can go against the word of the Lord! This is the way it's going to be—unless you surrender! If you..." Not able to finish, Jeremiah bowed his head and covered his face with his hands.

"I should never have come," Zedekiah turned to go.

Jeremiah looked up, his eyes full of tears. He closed them to think, then opened them with decision, "The Babylonians will come in full force!"

But even as the two men whispered their controversy, the Chaldeans were beginning to gather their equipment and retreat—of all things—retreat! Why? To go fight the Egyptians!

Jeremiah lay on his bed thinking, *Thank You, my Lord Father, for saving me and giving me some comfort once again. Thank You for sending my young Ethiopian friend. Please give the king a spirit of repentance. He seems to be wavering, and then he'll turn back again. Lord, please just help me to know what to do.* Sleep did not come easy.

The next day, Jeremiah's friends came to his quarters,

"The enemy is gathering their forces to go fight the Egyptian army and to prevent them from coming, at the king's request, to rescue Jerusalem."

Jeremiah said. "Zedekiah would do that. He will not be convinced that there is no help or hope from anywhere. When God speaks... the message will not change."

Jeremiah's fellow believers asked, "What can we do?"

Jeremiah thought for a moment and said, "As soon as the Chaldeans are gone, go by night into the temple and take the ark and hide it in a cave. The temple will be open for you. Prepare the ark for transport, with its staves and cover. Post lookouts at the gate and when everyone is asleep carry it quickly and quietly from the city into the country. Take it as far as you can and get it out of sight before dawn. You know this area. Be sure it is the most complicated cave you know of. Take it there, put it far into the deepest recesses, pack it in an orderly way, then seal it so it cannot be discovered. Then camouflage the entry to the cave. And I will pray for you."

When the Chaldeans retreated to fight the Egyptians, the servants of God took the ark and hid it. And so it is hidden from men's eyes to this very day.

The Babylonians did return. They destroyed the city, the gorgeous temple, and stole the golden furniture and all that pertained to its ceremonies. King Zedekiah lost his life. Jeremiah survived, staying in his own country to serve the remaining people left to farm the land. Eventually, Jeremiah, that faithful old prophet who said what the Lord had told him to say, was beaten to death by his own people.

CHAPTER 10

HISTORY'S CLIMAX

● ● ● ●

BC to AD 31...

I, Gabriel, will now continue my story of the progress of the terrible controversy between good and evil, although I observe that down in your time of history many call good evil, and evil good. But reality shows that the God of heaven has determined that His principles, even though hidden for centuries in the ark in a cave, shall survive forever—just like Himself.

Satan and his angel cohorts roamed the earth and other inhabited planets to try to deceive created beings into following him instead of God the Father who created him. But the inhabitants of the other planets totally rejected Satan and he no longer has access to any planets except Earth. What was it that happened to turn them against him so completely?

Right on time according to prophecy, God's Son was born of a virgin, in the right place, growing up in the right town, and becoming a Healer, Teacher, and a Prophet, fulfilling the words of all of God's prophets. But Satan nipped at His heels constantly.

For the first thirty years, Jesus grew up and worked as a carpenter, and because He was quiet, courteous, and cheerful, people didn't notice him, except for the fact that He was an unusually good young man in town. But at age thirty, things changed. At His baptism, God spoke to Him from heaven and launched Him as the Holy One of Israel who would save His people on Earth. Satan then tempted Him with fierce arguments.

We angels watched closely and recorded everything that went on. Because He taught practical goodness, honesty, purity, and lived it, the people loved Him, but the religious and political leaders began to resent

Him. They had to jealously guard their position and prestige by any and all means. As His popularity grew so did their hatred. He evaded their theological tricks and traps by exposing them and using it all to teach endearing lessons to the truth-hungry people.

Finally, after three-and-a-half years of Jesus' ministry of raising the dead, healing the sick, gently touching desperate lost lives, playing with the children, comforting mothers, and truly showing what God was like, the leaders had had enough. Conspiring to end His life by bribery and false witness, they went about making plans to capture Him.

We angels and our Father God suffered through it all, too, watching Him pray in the garden of Gethsemane at the foot of the Mount of Olives. Satan surrounded Him with evil angels and the blackness almost overcame Him. He had entered the place where he had become sinful humanity itself and was to take its punishment.

"Father, please take care of My disciples. They are not praying. They are sleeping. If they could know what this is all about it would help. But they are going into this without You. They think they have all the answers. They have not asked You for understanding. But please protect them and help them to come out of this without falling. And please take care of My people out there. They are honest in heart, but their hopes are all looking the wrong direction, in spite of all I've tried to teach them."

Satan looked down on Jesus' form bowed in agony and said, "Why do You worry about everybody? They don't care anything about You. The same people who followed You into the city singing Hosannas, and spreading palm branches, are the same ones who have cried 'Crucify Him!' Even Your disciples don't care enough to stay awake to help You when You need them. And why are You sweating blood? Your own nation's leaders hate You. Why are You crying like a baby? Stand up and walk away. Why should You care?"

At this Jesus collapsed prostrate on the ground, His face on the rough stones, His arms outstretched as if to embrace His Earth and to keep from being carried away by evil. "Father, if there is any way You can remove this cup from Me, please … But Thy will be done."

We angels watched. It seemed an eternity to us. Finally, He roused himself. Would He walk away? Would He stay?

"Thy will be done," He said, collapsing back to the ground. He chose to face the oncoming storm, knowing that He as fully man and fully God would give His life for all, from Adam to the last man on earth.

It was I, Gabriel, who took His fainting form in my arms, lifted His head to drink the bitter cup of sacrifice. He had made the most important choice ever made in history. His choice determined the destiny of the world.

CHAPTER 11

THE TWO PRIESTS

● ● ● ●

AD 31...

Here they come! Toward the dark, wooded mountain outside the city, with weapons of iron, with torches afire, they come: a mob of brigands, mercenaries, Roman soldiers, robed priests, among them the high priest, merchants, determined church officers. They reach the olive garden at the foot of the mountain where quietly burns a small fire, surrounded with wakening men, slowly, questioningly rising to their feet. Behind them a white-robed figure approaches the mob and asks whom they are seeking.

Jesus of Nazareth!

● ● ● ●

After years in the service of God in the temple, the two Jewish priests knew all the ceremonies thoroughly. They had been raised in the city of Jerusalem and had been ordained as priests. From the tribe of Levi, they served, teaching the people from the scrolls of the rabbis. They worked together much of the time. This day, their conversation might have gone something like this:

"He's back on the steps. And he's got a crowd out there, as if this were a special day," one said.

The court of the temple was filling up, and the Teacher from Galilee stood on the steps, speaking as if to each one, personally.

"He's good at telling stories. That's what holds the people," replied the other priest.

"Yes, and He's good at putting all us church workers in our place. He's nothing but trouble."

"Well, if He gets all the people to follow Him, we'll be out of a job."

"We can't let that happen."

"Caiaphas knows what he's doing to try to get rid of the rascal."

"But the teacher hasn't really done anything wrong. He's healed people, and some say He even raised a few dead people. That's hard to believe."

"Yes, but some of our rabbis were there and they saw the whole thing. 'Lazarus! Come out!' He said. And the man came from the tomb with his grave wrappings still on him! What, tell me, do we do with that?"

Things went smoothly that week until Thursday night. The chief priests were determined to get rid of the Prophet and had hired one of His followers to lead a contingent to capture Him.

"Well, there have been quite a few uprisings around here in the past few months and it could be He's using a different approach."

"Come on! It wasn't an act! Everybody there said it was genuine."

"Oh, what of it? Whether it's an act or not He's a menace to our whole system. They've got to get rid of Him some way."

"He's got quite a few pretty tough looking characters as His followers. And some are even so zealous they could cause a lot of damage. We have to be very careful. We are likely to be in the middle of a big uproar if things get any worse."

"But He just keeps preaching and telling stories. And He does have a lot of interesting and practical lessons to teach the people. And they seem to drink it in. And the kids love Him."

"Enough with the "ands." Come on—let's get to work. There are things that have to be done to get ready for the Passover."

Things went smoothly that week until Thursday night. The chief priests were determined to get rid of the Prophet and had hired one of

His followers to lead a contingent to capture Him. It had to be at night so the citizens would not be alarmed.

The two priests gathered with the group of ruffians, along with other priests and scribes late Thursday night. It was a motley group carrying torches and swords. The disciple, Judas by name, led the rabble, along with some of the elders, to capture the Teacher and bring Him back to the Sanhedrin to be tried.

The errand proved successful, although when the Teacher identified Himself saying, "I Am He," the two young priests—along with the whole crowd—fell backwards onto the ground, a mysterious power overcoming even the strongest of them.

The Teacher was interrogated endlessly, led from place to place for more questioning, made to answer for His leadership of the people, and two times beaten with scourges until His back was torn to shreds. All night, He was mocked, spit upon, and knocked around by the mob. Finally, Pilate, the Roman governor, at the insistence of the rabble, sentenced the Teacher to death by crucifixion. Pilate's own position and chances for promotion had been jeopardized, and he couldn't afford that.

That afternoon as the two priests came out and cleaned up for entering the temple, they prayed in their usual way to be worthy of this most sacred ceremony. This special Passover offering of the lamb, a yearly occasion, was to be slain as a symbol of the Messiah to come. Someday. Its blood must be taken into the most holy place and left there. For hundreds of years the golden chest with its precious contents—the tablets of stone with the Ten Commandments—had been absent, but the ceremony had continued. This blood offering was meant to cleanse the people of all their sins for the past year. All these rituals pointed forward to the promised Seed of the Woman whom the God of Heaven would send to save His people.

The two men talked together as they worked, finally picking out a sheep, making a final inspection to see if there were any blemishes or disease on it, and leading it into the court of the temple. Not all the people were outside the city watching the crucifixion; many of them had gathered for this ceremony in the court of the temple. It had grown suddenly dark over the city of Jerusalem, and now a distant rumble of thunder startled the two priests. A slight earth tremor shook under their feet. They continued their work of gathering their equipment, but as an eerie atmosphere surrounded them, they grew nervous.

Meanwhile, outside the city, a few people who had gathered to watch the execution of two criminals and the Teacher from Galilee were beginning to return early to the city with strange, sad looks on their faces, some beating their chests as if the distant thunder and far-off lightning had stricken them. The two priests watched in amazement. They had wondered at the outcome of the trial. They had stayed at the trial as long as they could and had watched the Teacher stand in regal calm as the rioters cast accusations and curses at Him. They both had felt embarrassed at the hatred of their leaders toward the man from Galilee who really had done nothing wrong. But now, this atmosphere of something tragic and mysterious hung on the air, giving the two a sense of foreboding. And where did this darkness come from?

Watching the crucifixion; many of them had gathered for this ceremony in the court of the temple. It had grown suddenly dark over the city of Jerusalem, and now a distant rumble of thunder startled the two priests. A slight earth tremor shook under their feet.

It was almost time. The priest gathered up the knife and the bowl for the blood, while his helper untied the lamb, kneeling down by the altar and holding the animal, who looked up at the priests with pleading eyes, trembling, but with no struggle. The razor-sharp knife was lifted to slit the animal's throat when suddenly the earth shook violently, followed by a deafening crash of thunder and instantaneous lightning. Terrifying screams sliced the atmosphere, the knife and bowl clattered to the floor, and the sheep dashed into the street. Then, a horrific tearing sound came from the most holy place. Looking up from their cowering position through the opening into the holy place, the two men gasped in fear as the great heavy curtain hiding the most holy place ripped in two from top to bottom! It was as if God had come down and ripped that heavy, sacred curtain with His own hands, opening to all who would venture inside its precincts. No longer the most holy place, no longer the dwelling place of the Shekinah, the Presence of God had left forever. The day of visitation had passed.

All nature seemed to explode, sending shivers down people's spines. Screeches and screams from the street turned to moans. Then a slow, heavy silence descended as if the earth had died. An atmosphere of hopelessness hovered over the city like a black cloud. Even the leaders who had conspired to kill Jesus came back into the city and returned to their families, but silent. It seemed that time had stopped. Everything had stopped.

CHAPTER 12

THE PRISON BREAK

● ● ● ●

AD 31...

The two soldiers left their barracks in the late afternoon. With clean uniforms and polished weapons, armor and shields, they strode from the city to join their legion for night guard duty.

The younger soldier shifted his shield to the other arm and frowned. Why did there have to be a hundred military men to guard a cemetery?

The other soldier watched the crowds streaming through the gate, his face etched in troubled thought. Pilate, the Roman governor, at the instigation of the suspicious priests, had posted an official guard at the tomb of the crucified "King of the Jews."

"If this character has an army hidden in the hills, they'll attack tonight, kidnap the body, and set up their own government with their own leader. And many of the people will follow," said one of them.

"But that would be suicide!" replied his friend. "They should know they can't conquer the Roman Empire!"

"But their 'king' has swayed thousands of people in such a short time. And all sorts of miracles have happened. It looks peaceful, but none should fool themselves."

The military guard had been assembled by their centurion, a tough yet clean man, and to the soldiers, amazingly, a gentleman. Looking impressive with his cape and red-crested helmet, he instructed his men to surround the cave where the victim was buried. "I'm warning you to neither sleep nor gamble. All are to remain silent in case the revolutionaries try to move in."

The two soldiers whispered as the troops fell out of line and reported to their post for the night; there would be no fun on this watch, for certain!

It was difficult not to sleep. It had been a hard couple of days and nights for all of them, trying to keep the hated Jews in line, especially on the Thursday night of their so-called "holy" weekend. Even during that night and into the next day, a crowd had formed and the celebrations continued, at times needing to be contained.

The two soldiers sat down together; in whispers they tried to put a bit of this nonsense into some kind of perspective. They looked up at the cave where the famous victim, Jesus of Nazareth, was lying dead, betrayed by His own people. A huge rock at the door of the cave had been securely fastened to the rock behind by cords and the Roman seal.

One of them softly murmured, "Most of his enemies are leaders, jealous and determined to keep their power. The common people liked Him though, as long as there was a chance of Him becoming their king. Who wouldn't be interested in a king that could feed five thousand people from just a few loaves and fishes? And He even acted like a king, a good one at that ... so dignified, yet compassionate toward suffering people. He dressed like a commoner, yet royalty shone from the way He acted." It was all too complicated to even try to understand.

The night wore on. Nothing happened. Only quiet conversation and disturbing thoughts filled their minds with the part they had played in the prolonged trial, the lashing with a scourge which tore the poor man's back to pieces, the mockery of Him as "king," clothed in the jeweled velvet robe soaked in blood, and crowned with a ring of two-inch thorns. Then there was the long, slow, tumultuous journey from the city as He passed out a couple of times trying to carry the heavy cross beam, until somebody helped Him. The ridicule and final execution of that gentle, yet regal Man, now lying dead in the sealed cave before them, echoed in their brains all night. Those regrets prevented any kind of sleep, even if they'd tried.

They thought of what their centurion had exclaimed when Jesus died amidst thunders and lightnings. An earthquake had broken huge boulders and sent them rolling down the hills. He had stood transfixed, staring at the dead form on the cross, and exclaimed, "Surely, He *was* the Son of God!"

Having rested through the day, the large company of soldiers kept faithful guard. Another company had overseen the crowds on the Jews' holy Sabbath, and had reported that somehow, the atmosphere in the city had been eerily quiet and mournful. In the years before, during this holy day, all the people had enjoyed worshipping, feasting, and visiting together. But today there seemed to be an atmosphere of mysterious premonition—something they couldn't quite explain.

"Maybe things will get back to normal by tomorrow," one of the soldiers murmured.

One guard rose to his feet, walking a short distance to keep awake, then walking back, thinking as he paced.

About 4:00 in the morning, the soldiers, now relaxed, some talking quietly, others becoming sleepy, began to see the mist of dawn. The earth rumbled slightly. They raised their heads. Not another one! Memories returned of the day of the crucifixion. Another rumble. Lightning flashed and thunder rolled in the distance.

Suddenly an explosion of lightning shook them to the ground. A brilliant light illuminated the whole area. The guards struggled to their feet.

What....?

"Look!" The soldiers leaned forward. A brilliant, fiery being descended to the tomb, and with superhuman strength rolled aside the huge, sealed stone as if it were made of paper.

The angel shouted out in triumph, "Master! Come forth! Your Father calls Thee!"

All the soldiers gaped in awe, their spears and shields forgotten. Suddenly the earth shook violently, lightning striking close by and deafening thunder knocked them to the ground again. From inside the dark tomb, there flashed a blinding light. The earth convulsed once again.

Cries of terror and amazement came from the soldiers' mouths as slowly the Victim appeared in the doorway, no longer wrapped in grave clothes, but in soft clothing of warm light. His face shone like the sun.

He smiled and with open face, lifted His arms and eyes upward toward heaven. "My Father, I come! I AM the resurrection and the life!"

Then he stared down at the guards. Armor clashed against metal as each soldier fell backward, unconscious, against his companion, domino-like, until they formed a heap of rubble, tangled and paralyzed.

By the time they regained their senses, Jesus had disappeared. The soldiers ran this way and that, shouting at each other, bumping into each other. Some ran into the city, forgetting their weapons, forgetting they were still on duty.

The centurion, trying to keep his voice calm, ordered those that remained to go with him to tell the governor. The Jews' victim has risen! The two soldiers followed the centurion and a few other guards to report to Pilate. But intersecting them in the way came a messenger from the high priest, Caiaphus, summoning them to his sumptuous quarters in the city.

Caiaphus, disturbed in his sleep for the second time in three days, grunted his annoyance at the disturbance. Someone had burst into quarters to tell him the news. At learning that his plans were foiled, he stared into space, his pale lips moving but making no sound. Then, finally, he shouted to summon the guard. "They'll pay for this!"

At learning that his plans were foiled, he stared into space, his pale lips moving but making no sound. Then, finally, he shouted to summon the guard. "They'll pay for this!"

It was a shaken and disheveled group of Roman warriors who staggered into the presence of the leader of the Jewish nation. "We saw Him!" they stammered. "It was so bright! And we heard singing!" Each man gave his testimony with trembling face and tongue.

The high priest, by now joined by other rulers and scribes, stood shaking, not knowing what to do. The soldiers began to leave.

"Wait! Wait! Your men are to say He was stolen from the grave!"

The centurion whirled around, angry, "What did you say?"

"You are to say He was stolen while you slept!"

"Our soldiers did not sleep! It took many strong hands to place that stone and seal it, and you expect us to say it was removed the same way without a hundred soldiers knowing it? Absolutely not!"

"Just do it!" cried the high priest.

The centurion's eyes flashed with anger. "Does this mean that all my brave men will be executed for failing their mission?"

"No, No, No!" the high priest's voice rose with impatience. "We'll ask for them to be spared. You will not be punished!"

"Is this just a promise from you? What about your friends?" The centurion's voice sounded strangely challenging.

"Yes! Yes! They will agree with me! We will talk with Pilate. He will agree. We will pay your men!" The face of Caiaphus was contorted with fear and rage.

As the soldiers later exited with their bribes, and entered the street, the centurion murmured, "It will never work! The word is out now. They've not only murdered their king; they've covered it up with money. They're fighting a losing battle! And the Roman army will never be the same!" He threw his hush money to the ground and mumbled under his breath, "The anger and hatred of the guilty knows no limits. Curse them!"

He stopped suddenly, staring at the street before him, then with confidence and a tone of victory filling his voice, he cried. "He WAS the Messiah! He IS God's Son! ...God help us!" He turned to his young companions and said, "I believe that now! I believe it!"

After a moment of deep thought he said, "None of us can deny it. No matter how much money they try to pay us!"

The two soldiers nodded their heads with conviction. They stared around at the streets of Jerusalem, now filling with early morning risers who had been awakened by the lightning strikes and shaking earth. "As unbelievable as it is, we can't believe anything else! We saw it with our own eyes!"

● ● ● ●

And sure enough, Jesus the Christ not only won the victory over Satan in proving His love for His Creation, but He conquered death as well!

From this dramatic event, Christ stayed for forty days with His followers to train them and give them a deeper vision of their responsibilities. In spite of the disbelief and continued opposition of the Jewish leaders, the Good News spread like wildfire.

The fact that the Roman Empire continued to rule the Jewish nation for more than another 300 years, when it fell in AD 476, further embittered the populace, but the power of grace dwelt in the hearts of the believers who encouraged everyone to consider and believe.

CHAPTER 13

JOHN THE REVELATOR

● ● ● ●

AD 96...

The prisoner, clad in a simple robe and sandals, struggled to keep his balance as the guards kicked and pushed him out the door into the prison yard, then out the gate into the street. His public execution would warn the people against joining this revolutionary movement that had blown through the populace of southern Europe and the Middle East like a gale, giving them hope of change. As the victim approached the crowded city square of Rome, he gasped as he saw smoke rising from a huge fire under a large steaming caldron.

His defense had been simple and eloquent, filled with truth and perfect reasoning, which angered his enemies, especially Domitian, the emperor, who, in his rage, condemned this humble servant of God to death in boiling oil.

"Thus perish all who believe in that deceiver, Jesus Christ of Nazareth!" shouted John's enemies.

John had declared, "My Master patiently submitted to all that Satan and his angels could devise to humiliate and torture Him. He gave His life to save the world. I am honored in being permitted to suffer for His sake. I am a weak, sinful man. Jesus Christ, only, was holy, harmless, undefiled. He did no sin, neither was guile found in His mouth."

With this, Roman soldiers picked him up and threw him into the boiling oil, splashing a bit on themselves. Sounds of horror burst from the crowd, but the victim slowly regained his feet and stood unharmed. The groans turned to shouts of amazement. "He's alive! It can't be!" His face reflected gratitude to his Savior who hundreds of years before had walked with the three Hebrew worthies in the fiery furnace and they had emerged without even the smell of smoke on them. Many cowered from the caldron, but John returned to his quarters with more friends than when he came. Many stayed far into the night, asking questions and studying the scriptures with him. Another victory won!

Amazed and humbled, but unrepentant, the Jewish leaders and the emperor decided the best they could do was to banish him somewhere, so his influence could no longer reach the people who now considered him a hero.

Patmos, a barren, rocky island in the Aegean Sea, the inescapable prison for recalcitrant criminals, then became the home of the apostle, John. However, on lonely Patmos, John still won desperate souls to Christ, and experienced the greatest joy of his life, as the Lord Himself and the holy angels came to be his companions. But let John tell his story:

On lonely Patmos, John still won desperate souls to Christ, and experienced the greatest joy of his life, as the Lord Himself and the holy angels came to be his companions.

"Sitting on this mountain, I thought of Moses sitting atop Mt. Sinai, more than 1,500 miles to the southeast, and almost two thousand years ago. My habit since I arrived has been to climb up here to be alone with God on the seventh day of the week, the Lord's Day. I desire to enter into His rest after a week of living and laboring in the mines with these restless criminals on the island. I am a miracle of long life, more than eighty years, changed by three-and-a-half years with the world's Creator and Redeemer. I cared for Jesus' mother, Mary, after His crucifixion. I gave the Good News not only to Jews, but also to Gentiles, and saw their radiant faces as they realized they were accepted by heaven. I have observed their changed lives—lives transformed by the power of the written Word and the Holy Spirit. I survived the caldron of boiling oil. I have met and dealt with opposition, hatred, and conspiracies, yet the Lord has given me peace.

"As the Mediterranean sun beams into every crevice of the rocks here, I have brought writing material and the scripture rolls. I like to talk to my Lord and to read and write. It helps me to sort out the issues at hand. A gentle breeze fanned me that day as I sat down on one of the volcanic boulders that lay scattered here on the island. Looking out over the sea on all sides, I felt peace in this world of chaos. With my eyes closed, my mind wandered over the past. As one of the "sons of thunder" back in my home town, learning how to work hard at the fishermen's trade, I met Jesus and became one of His helpers along with my brother, James. Our mother joyfully expected us to be the Messiah's righthand men after the great revolution, but then she became bitterly disappointed at the cross, like all of us.

"But the miraculous resurrection and ascension of Jesus changed everything. Now the Good News of salvation to all people must be preached to the world. Soon the promise of the great resurrection of the righteous dead at the second coming of Jesus to Earth will be fulfilled. Then I will again see my brother James, who was beheaded in prison at the command of the wicked Herod Agrippa I.

"Suddenly a super-bright light penetrated my closed eyes and my mind; a voice came down from heaven. Yes! It was a familiar voice—that of Jesus, my beloved Master—but it had an ethereal sound like faraway trumpets, like a waterfall, like winds whirling around in a deep chasm.

"And I turned to see the voice that spoke with me … one like the Son of Man, clothed with a garment down to the foot, and girded about the middle with a golden belt. His hair was white as snow and His eyes were as flames of fire. And His feet were like fine brass as if they burned in a furnace, and His voice as the sound of many waters. When I saw Him, I fell at His feet as dead. He laid His right hand upon me saying unto me, 'Fear not: I am the First and the Last. I am He that liveth, and was dead, and, behold, I am alive for evermore … Write the things which you have seen, and things which are, and things which shall be hereafter.'

"So the Lord showed me scenes portraying the history of the Christian church down through the ages to the end of time when He, as King of Kings, will come from heaven to Earth to rescue His people who have kept His word in spite of persecution and death.

"And there was given me a reed like unto a rod; and the angel stood, saying, 'Rise and measure the temple of God, and the altar, and them that worship therein.' The temple in heaven appeared many times during my vision. I saw the throne as housed in the temple, the court, the altar, the priests, the Lamb, the door, pillars, and the veil. On the inside I saw the candlestick, the golden altar, and censer. I saw God upon His great, white throne above the ark, the magnificent golden ark. It took my breath away. All were larger, more colorful, more exquisite than the original built in the wilderness ... more magnificent than even Solomon's temple.

"I saw the terrible spiritual battle with Satan and how he had succeeded in destroying humanity. I saw the gorgeous creation made by a simple word from the lips of the Master, and how this enemy had instigated the destruction of its beauty.

"I saw this horrific fight progressing to the place where even the Christian churches had taken political power to legislate laws, making man-made laws look more important than God's eternal laws. They made unity look wonderful, even though based on lies. This furious controversy will end only when Christ comes back. The enemy will even appear as Christ Himself and by subtle flatteries destroy many.

"The angel guided me through visions, explaining to me some of what they mean. The entire spectrum of Christian history was laid out before me. I couldn't begin to understand it, but I was not asked to understand—I was only told to write it down. I'm like Daniel: he didn't understand either, what the beasts and the symbolism all meant, but his prophetic visions coincide marvelously with the ones I received!

"What an experience! To see the temple of God in heaven! To see Jesus interceding for His people, to see the heavenly ark, the great pattern for the earthly ark still hidden somewhere in a cave.

"Even after I gained freedom from my island prison, and returned to my life in Asia Minor, I thought so often of that magnificent series of visions, the deepest honor of seeing my Lord again. Someday we'll all be together."

CHAPTER 14

LIGHT IN THE DARKNESS—
HIRAM EDSON

● ● ● ●

October 1844...

The sun shone brightly through the bedroom window that morning of October 23rd. Hiram and his wife, Esther, were tired—they had wept and prayed all night with their friends downstairs. At dawn everyone had gone home. And now the two lay in bed thinking. It was much past their usual rising time. There were no animals to feed. All the garden vegetables had been given away. There had been only a few potatoes left in the patch. They lay silently staring at the ceiling. There didn't seem to be any reason to get up. It was not going to be a good day.

What are the neighbors going to say? Oh, they would say, "We told you the Lord was not going to come! How stupid can you be?"

It was that way in quite a few homes that morning. They had thought Jesus would come yesterday. The Bible prophecy had said the sanctuary would be cleansed at the end of the time period described in Daniel 8:14. The believers around the world, from people of all beliefs who had studied the prophecy, were certain He would come in great triumph. The excitement was almost universal. Many citizens from countries around the globe expressed their new belief in Christ and had committed themselves in loyalty to Him.

But October 22 had come and gone, and Jesus had not appeared. What a disappointment! Most of the new "believers" left as quickly as they had come.

And now the Edsons had to face their neighbors who had ridiculed them before. They would say, "We told you Jesus said, 'No man knoweth the day or hour but My Father in heaven!' We told you! Now what are you going to do?"

But what other people thought was not the worst thing. Were their hopes in vain? Were the scriptures deceiving them? Didn't God care? Was there even a God?

"Of course God is there. We know He's with us, but how could He do this to us?"

Finally, Hiram struggled up and sat on the side of the bed. He could feel the cold. "Well, we'll just have to go back to studying the whole thing over again and see where we went wrong. We'll need to get together with our friends some more and work it through. We can't just give up. The Bible is true; somehow, we've gotten it wrong."

So after their breakfast of potatoes, Hiram and his friend, Owen Crosier, trudged through a corn field, still with corn shocks in it, toward the neighbor's barn where the men usually met to study and pray.

"Maybe some of them will be there. As tired as we are, we can't sleep anyway; we might as well study some more and see where we went wrong. God has not left us. I know He…"

Suddenly Hiram stopped, but Crosier went on. It was as if a hand had touched Hiram's shoulder. He heard a voice: "The sanctuary is in heaven." He looked up into the sky and saw in his mind's eye Christ, clothed as High Priest with the jeweled breastplate on His chest, officiating before the ark of the covenant!

In heaven! Not earth! He's gone into the Most Holy Place! The Day of Atonement! The cleansing of the sanctuary in heaven!

Falling to his knees on the cold ground, Hiram lifted his folded hands to heaven, "Oh, Thank You, Lord! Thank You! Thank You!"

Jumping up, he began running, stumbling on clods and cut corn stalks, toward the barn where he found his friends sitting around on hay bales and upturned buckets with their Bibles, turning the pages, asking questions of each other, looking up at him with pale, haggard faces.

They had been studying since dawn, comparing scripture with scripture, praying together, encouraging those whose neighbors or families had rejected them. Quoting scripture promises, each man gained courage, then he would convey it to the others. "He that endureth to the end shall be saved!" "Be strong and of good courage..." "He that will come, shall come." "Behold, I come quickly, and my reward is with Me to give to every man according as his work shall be."

Rushing into the barn panting, Hiram shouted the great news, "I see it now! I've seen Jesus!" He stood holding his Bible out at arm's length. "It's in here! He's the High Priest standing before the ark! The cleansing of the sanctuary! It's in heaven! Not the earth!"

His friends jumped to their feet, gathering around him. Hiram repeated, "I saw Him! He's dressed as High Priest standing before the ark!"

"Of course! Why didn't we think of that? The cleansing of the sanctuary in heaven!"

Hiram stood in the midst of his friends and explained, "Can you see it? Christ dressed all in white from His head down, on His head a large, white headdress with a metal plate on His forehead. And He has jewels on His front: the breastplate, covered with jewels, all colors and they sparkle!"

"Hebrews! That's where it is! It's all in Hebrews!" Crosier shouted.

The men quickly picked up their Bibles, sat down, and turned to the passages in Hebrews 9 that describe Christ as the great High Priest ministering in the heavenly sanctuary. All the sins that were brought into the holy place during the year were transferred to the ark of the covenant and the mercy seat on the Day of Atonement! And John saw the ark in the heavenly sanctuary! Revelation!

A thorough study of Hebrews, the Old Testament, and Revelation, as well as Daniel, revealed the present significance of Christ's judgment and intercession, and finally satisfied those devout Bible scholars.

On his return home late that afternoon, Hiram's wife Esther reached for his hands at the news. He held her close. "The ridicule means nothing now. The meaning is clear. The book of Hebrews proves that!" He sat down at the kitchen table. "And the book of Revelation—it's amazing. Once again, the New Testament has illuminated the Old Testament and the Old Testament, the New!"

Esther sighed deeply, looked far away, shook her head, closed her eyes, and finally smiled. So many mixed emotions.

Because most of the advent believers had been so bitterly disappointed, they either went back to their churches or stopped going to church altogether. Out of the thousands of people around the world who looked for Christ to come, only about fifty remained who took courage and went back to their Bibles. God had not left His people! Today they number in the millions!

These faithful believers, during the months that followed, studied the doctrine of the sanctuary. This Bible teaching made clear the meaning of the shed blood of Christ, and the reason for His death. And now, serving as Great High Priest, the Ambassador from heaven to Earth, and at the same time representing Earth to heaven, Christ proved His loyalty to his faithful followers.

Studying the subject of the Day of Atonement, the believers learned many things that were significant to their own situation: The early Israelites were taught to clean themselves and their homes, to get rid of all trash, and make things right with their neighbors before the great day of the yearly sacrifice. That was of utmost importance. And now in the heavenly sanctuary the judgment had arrived, and the records of all would be reviewed.

Hiram and his wife reasoned through the new teaching. Hiram murmured, "Well, if we aren't clean, we'll never get there! But thank God, He's provided a way, so our records are cleansed. Thank You, Lord!" He looked out the window. "Then, because we're free now and so grateful, and love Him so much, we serve Him and follow Him wherever He leads us".

Esther exclaimed, "The New Covenant! He's written the law in our hearts!"

Hiram and his wife at that moment gained new courage and went out, with faces lit up, to give the new Good News to their neighbors and friends. Meanwhile, through those troubled days, and many years since, inside the earthly ark of the covenant, lay the tables of stone, the universal principles of right living, hidden somewhere in a cave. They are the copy of the great pattern from heaven, given to Moses on Sinai. But above, covering the Ten Commandments, is solid gold, and the Presence of a merciful God.

CHAPTER 15

THE ROCK THAT CHANGED A LITTLE GIRL'S LIFE

● ● ● ●

1836...

With long curls bouncing, with school books dangling dangerously, with feet and legs running as fast as three little girls could make them go, the distance into town shortened by the second. A fourth girl running behind picked up a rock.

Hurry! The stores can offer some protection if reached in time. As one of the girls looked back, the large stone hurtled through the air and struck her in the face. Time stood still. Crumbling to the ground, blood spurting from her flattened nose, little Ellen fainted.

Thus, a case of early 19th century bullying launched the career of one little girl chosen by God to take messages of instruction and encouragement to a fledgling church that today numbers over nineteen million members in the fastest growing Protestant church in the world.

Later, the little girl's father, wearied from several weeks away and a long trip home, quickly fed and watered his horse, pulled the small carriage in from the weather, and hurried anxiously toward the farmhouse. His beloved wife and children ran out on the porch to greet him with hugs and kisses.

How the children had grown in such a short time! They crowded into the kitchen all chattering at once. He hugged each one while they beamed at him. And yet ... there was something uncomfortable at the same time. Something was wrong. Somehow, he could feel a cloud hovering over his little family. How many? Six, seven ... yes, someone was missing. He looked around the room, then at Mother. Ellen! Where was Ellen? Their joyous faces turned serious as Mother murmured Ellen's whereabouts, pointing toward the pantry.

"In the pantry? Why?" Father stepped toward the pantry. Then his face paled as his nine-year-old daughter came out into the kitchen. His voice broke as he spoke her name. "Ellen!" He dropped to his knees and took her gently by the shoulders. The once bouncy, beautiful child bowed her head, trying to hide a terribly disfigured face, and the tears that streamed down her scarred cheeks. Her nose had been flattened into her face, and still showed fresh red scars. Her eyes, still blackened, pleaded for understanding and comfort, "Daddy!"

"What happened?" He choked back a father's cry as his fingers touched her face. The child sobbed and fell into his arms. He held her close, caressing her hair as her frail body shook in his embrace.

Ellen's twin sister, Elizabeth, came close. Father drew her in. Elizabeth wanted to explain to him what had happened, "That older girl at school who liked to tease us, worried us almost every day. Mother told us to run home if she started getting mean. So on that day, the girl began to chase us, shouting hateful words. Ellen had looked back to see how close she was, and just then the girl threw a rock and hit Ellen right in the face!"

She had fallen to the ground bleeding profusely. The girl had run away quickly. Another girlfriend and Elizabeth had tried to pick Ellen up but she could only struggle to her feet and limp as the girls guided her into a nearby store. People tried to help, but she didn't want to get blood on them. A man even offered to take her home in his carriage, but she wouldn't go with him because she didn't want to get blood inside his carriage.

Elizabeth began to cry. Father held both his twins and looked at Mother.

Mother then explained, "This happened weeks ago. The doctor has been to see Ellen several times and has expressed surprise that she's still alive. You can see how much weight she's lost. She's been so sick, and we didn't know how to get in touch with you."

Father, still on his knees, smoothed their tousled heads. Then as he stood to his feet, a determined look on his face sent a message to them all. Now was the time to live above this thing, "I promise you Ellen, we'll all do everything we can to help you get well, and to succeed in life in spite of this. There was some good reason why God allowed this to happen, and you will just have to trust Him. He will lead you and make you one of His servants." Father radiated quiet confidence that cheered them all, "You must put yourself in God's care. And prayer always helps. Let's talk to Him now about this whole thing."

> *"I promise you Ellen, we'll all do everything we can to help you get well, and to succeed in life in spite of this. There was some good reason why God allowed this to happen, and you will just have to trust Him. He will lead you and make you one of His servants."*

The family fell to their knees as they had so many times before under better circumstances, and Father raised his face and voice toward the God of Heaven. It might have gone something like this:

"Oh, Father, thank you for this fine family. Thank you for bringing me home again. Thank you that You have always kept us and cared for us. We don't know why this has happened to our little girl. We have tried to do things right, but we fail all too often. Please, may Your healing, forgiving Spirit come down and make things all right for Ellen. And please forgive the schoolmate who did this to her. We are sure she must feel bad, too. Give us all a forgiving spirit and help us to be a blessing to her and her family in the weeks and months ahead. We claim Your promise that all things work together for good to those who love You and are called according to Your purpose. Please make this child of Yours well again and heal us all. In Jesus' name, amen."

Ellen's face never regained its original beauty. Medical science in the 1830s and 40s barely met the needs of those with traumatic injuries. As Ellen grew into her teens, her face, though scarred, grew less unsightly. The human body heals miraculously, but in this case, Ellen, always energetic and intelligent, was never to know complete health again. Her school teachers, after a few weeks of watching Ellen in her futile attempts at studying and writing, advised her parents to remove her from school. To Ellen, this was the greatest blow of all.

After months of spiritual struggle, Ellen became a devoted Christian. She spent much time alone with the Lord trying to meet the challenges of her handicap. The family belonged to the Methodist church and Ellen loved to study the Bible. She joined women's study groups and prayer sessions. Even at her tender age, her serious, thoughtful demeanor endeared her to the older women.

At the age of seventeen she still suffered ill health, but one day as she knelt with a group of ladies for worship and prayer, Ellen suddenly did not move.

"Ellen! Ellen!" The women stood to their feet and called out to her, but Ellen, as if frozen on her knees, with her hands outstretched and her eyes open, could not respond. What has happened? Is she dead? They stared, trembling in wonder.

"She doesn't seem to be breathing!"

"If she has died, though, wouldn't she fall over?" So her friends watched her there until she moved.

"Ellen! Ellen! Are you all right?" They gathered closer, helping her to her feet and sitting her in a chair.

Her face glowed, "I ... I had a dream! It ... it was beautiful—but so frightening!" She looked around the room as if she couldn't believe she was there and then her face clouded, and she began to cry.

"There, there, child, you're all right now." One of the ladies put her own sweater around Ellen's shoulders.

"I raised my eyes, and saw a straight and narrow path, cast up high above the world. On this path the Advent people were traveling to the city, which was at the farther end of the path. They had a bright light set up behind them at the beginning of the path, which an angel told me was the midnight cry. This light shone all along the path and gave light for their feet so that they might not stumble. If they kept their eyes fixed on Jesus, who was just before them, leading them to the city, they were safe. But soon some grew weary, and said the city was a great way off, and they expected to have entered it before. Then Jesus would encourage them by raising His glorious right arm, and from His arm came a light which waved over the Advent band, and they shouted, 'Alleluia!' Others rashly denied the light behind them, and said that it was not God that had led them out so far. The light behind them went out, leaving their feet in perfect darkness, and they stumbled and lost sight of the mark and of Jesus, and fell off the path down into the dark and wicked world below. Soon we heard the voice of God like many waters, which gave us the day and hour of Jesus' coming. The living saints, 144,000 in number, knew and understood the voice, while the wicked thought it was thunder and an earthquake..."

Through the months and years, Father's prayer was answered. Forgiveness and peace reigned between the families of Ellen and the girl who threw the rock. In fact, this young lady helped Ellen study. Ellen soon learned to read and write. Amazingly, with only a few grades of formal education, she is credited with writing many books, translated into the most languages, and has been declared by the United States Library of Congress as the writer of the most authoritative and spiritually compelling treatise on the life of Christ.

God answered her father's prayer in another miraculous way: He gave her a career of conveying messages to His people, messages not only of encouragement, but of rebuke and correction. She fulfilled all the qualifications put forth by the Bible for her prophetic work. During visions she did not breathe, had her eyes open, could not be moved, sometimes spoke, but with her own gentle sweet voice. During her visions, she could turn to texts of scripture without looking, and quote them, and often saw in vision councils in session, churches, and other organizations struggling with error, people's personal lives, or a landmark that indicated the future location of a hospital or college. Then she would write down what she saw. The vision would prove true, sometimes in spite of denial or opposition, but true in the end.

Her own personal life imitated the best of godly women, loving her husband, children, and home, raising a garden, sewing, cooking, and cleaning. Although she preferred to stay home and take care of her family, she was called to travel often and went only because God had called her to go.

One morning Ellen, at her home, had sat up most of the night writing out what she had seen in her dreams and visions. This morning she groaned inwardly as she rose from her desk chair, yet her eyes shone as she watched out the window at the dawn. She lifted her head as daylight greeted her. She had written as fast as she could through the night, dipping her pen into the inkwell only as the last drop of ink faded. Her latest dream had left her weak but excited, and she determined that it must be written down immediately.

Among the many things that God had shown her was the building of the original tabernacle, the adventures in the history of the ark of the covenant, how it was built, and later hidden in a cave. She was shown how Christ fulfilled all the symbolism in the sanctuary service. He was not only the High Priest, but the Lamb, sacrificed for all the sins of mankind.

Many years later, toward the end of her long ministry, Ellen saw in vision the last days before Christ would come in the clouds. The wicked who had tried to destroy God's commandment-keeping people in one night, around the world, stared into the sky with fear as the golden chest opened in panorama before the inhabitants of Earth, showing the Ten Commandments in their original glory.

After more than seventy years of labor, much of it in poverty, having to leave the comfort of home and family, Ellen triumphed in seeing the numbers of believers grow. Unlike the fearful seventeen-year-old invalid she had been, she rejoiced in the strength, ability, and courage the Lord had given her through the years, and in seeing honest souls come out of darkness into the light of everlasting Bible truth.

CHAPTER 16

THE TWO LAWS

● ● ● ●

The Ten Commandments—Eternal Principles for All Humanity

These were written in stone by the finger of God and were housed inside the golden chest. They are what made the ark holy.

1. You must not have any other gods but me.
2. You must not make for yourself an idol of any kind or an image of anything in the heavens or on the earth or in the sea. You must not bow down to them or worship them, for I, the Lord your God, am a jealous God, who will not tolerate your affection for any other gods. I lay the sins of the parents upon their children. The entire family is affected—even children in the third and fourth generations of those who reject Me. But I lavish unfailing love for thousands of them who love Me and obey My commands.
3. You must not misuse the name of the Lord your God. The Lord will not let you go unpunished if you misuse His name.
4. Remember to observe the Sabbath day by keeping it holy. You have six days every week for your ordinary work, but the seventh day is a Sabbath day of rest dedicated to the Lord your God. On that day no one in your household may do any work. This includes you, your sons and daughters, your male and female servants, your livestock, and any foreigners living among you. For in six days the Lord made the heavens, the earth, the sea, and everything in them; but on the seventh day

He rested. That is why the Lord blessed the Sabbath day and set it apart as holy.

5. Honor your father and mother. Then you will live a long, full life in the land the Lord your God is giving you.
6. You must not murder.
7. You must not commit adultery.
8. You must not steal.
9. You must not testify falsely against your neighbor.
10. You must not covet your neighbor's house. You must not covet your neighbor's wife, male or female servant, ox or donkey, or anything else that belongs to your neighbor.

The Ceremonial Law
(Written on scrolls by Moses and kept outside of the ark)

Among the statutes and laws Moses received during his six-week sojourn on Sinai was God's description of the sacrificial system required to symbolize His own sacrifice for His people. This law is the one that was nailed to the cross; in other words, Jesus' sacrifice fulfilled this law.

> *If a person committed a sin, that is if he broke one of the Ten Commandments, the punishment would be eternal death, but the blood of a lamb would substitute for his own life.*

Back in the beginning, after Adam had chosen to eat the fruit of the forbidden tree, thereby betraying his Creator, God said to bring lambs without blemish. If a person committed a sin, that is if he broke one of the Ten Commandments, the punishment would be eternal death, but the blood of a lamb would substitute for his own life. The result of sin is death and the lamb would die in the sinner's place.

Its death prefigured the sacrifice that God's Son would give for the sins of humanity.

Offerings of food, such as grain, were part of the sanctuary service as thank offerings for a good harvest. These food offerings celebrated God's goodness in providing sustenance and protection. While God did not need any of these sacrifices and offerings, they reminded the people of their need of Him, of their own needs, and of the final sacrifice of their Creator and Redeemer.

CHAPTER 17

WHERE WILL YOU END UP?

● ● ● ●

Today and beyond...

A drone hovers quietly overhead. Infra-red lights penetrate the darkness. Insects and creatures of the night cease singing and calling. A group of campers hunker down in their sleeping bags waiting, waiting. It's certain their camp will be spotted in spite of their precautions, having camouflaged the site as best they could. You and your wife lay still, holding each other's hand, waiting, listening.

How long have you been here in this wooded place? Maybe two months? Leaving home in your small village in the north, having disconnected your GPS, cell phones, and other devices, you joined your friends and traveled in an old van to the interior reaches of the mountains as far as the road went. Using all your camping skills in packing food and supplies, you left your van in an abandoned barn, and hiked into this remote site and camped here for several weeks.

Each of the couples have separated from each other so if one is spotted, the others can't be found, covering tents completely with greenery, hiding supplies underground, and meeting only once during a three- or four-day period to report, to read the Bible, to pray together, and encourage each other. You prayed in years past that your "flight" would not be in the winter, as Christ had instructed in Matthew 24, and now you are thankful for His answer to that prayer. Even though the summer nights are cold here, it's not winter when it can drop to thirty or forty degrees below zero.

All your survival skills come to the forefront. Dehydrated food and foraging for edible plants have made your exile more tolerable. The small, solar-powered radio keeps you informed of the latest news which isn't good, yet is good. The worse the news sounds, the nearer your rescue will be.

Suddenly you hear the sound of branches and sticks breaking underfoot and voices saying quietly, "Over here!" Soon your tent is being slashed open with knives, and the two of you are exposed to four troopers pointing at you with guns.

"Get up! You're coming with us!" You are led about half a mile to a camp. The military has stationed men to find any runaway "fanatics" and bring them back to jail. A new prison in a nearby town in the county is to hold "the whole lot of them," as one judge had ordered. Even though the place was newly built in the center of town, secrecy had prevailed. It had been publicized as "security" for illegal immigrants. You have heard of this prison, though, where the believers have been treated in a way that makes Abu Ghraib sound like kindergarten.

The hardest part of entering into this place is that the two of you must be separated. Your wife's lips quiver a "God bless you, I love you!" as she is taken one way and you another. There are plenty of both men and women in both directions, calculated only to weaken the resolve and moral integrity of all the inmates.

You lost your radio in the foray, but the guards keep you informed of the news. "People like you are the cause of all this trouble!" they sneer. More cities have been wiped from the face of the earth by earthquakes, floods, terrorist attacks, and tsunamis; fires rage over millions of acres of plain and forest; the financial situation in the world has completely collapsed; ordinary law-abiding people break into their neighbors' homes to find food. Everywhere around the world, safety is a thing of the past. Crowds and mobs roam the streets of the cities vandalizing shops, stores, private homes, hospitals, even nursing homes. The old atomic and nuclear bombs, hidden for decades, destroy the largest cities in the world.

Why are all these people in prison? Because they refuse to work on the seventh day of the week, Saturday. "It's not important what day you keep" has been taught for centuries, but now suddenly, by federal and One World law, things have changed drastically. So, you and your wife, somewhere in the deep recesses of this prison, are "housed" along with other violators of a law that "isn't important."

You are also convicted of "hate crimes." Though you hate no one, you have taught the Bible prophecies that tell of gross errors in large churches that try to force false man-made doctrines upon those who prefer to think for themselves. Bible prophecy is fast fulfilling.

The days pass. You see nothing of your camping companions. Maybe they were not discovered. There are a few caves in the mountains; hopefully, they were able to hide in places like that. Who knows?

The day has come. Two grim-faced officers escort you into the sparsely filled courtroom, a part of the building where you have resided the last month without legal advice or visitors. Your

Everywhere around the world, safety is a thing of the past. Crowds and mobs roam the streets of the cities vandalizing shops, stores, private homes, hospitals, even nursing homes. The old atomic and nuclear bombs, hidden for decades, destroy the largest cities in the world.

family has ignored you, which you expect, since they have treated you politely but coolly since you moved back to your hometown two years ago, having left a successful business in the city for peaceful, small-town living. Thinking you would fare better in a small place, and hoping you might be able to work at your occupation without prejudice, you came home, but the same conditions existed here. Now the law of the land has changed, and you cannot live your life as you wish, following the Bible and obeying God as you believe you should.

Now you have been accused of the crime of breaking the Sunday law which was passed a few months ago by the federal government, which was said to please God because He wanted everyone united under one code. They have tried for months to destroy all the Bibles, going from house to house searching and burning. Even the U.S. President has ordered military Bibles to be burned, but the Bible is still the perfect rule of faith, and you have refused to work on Saturday. So you were arrested, and have spent weeks behind bars trying to be decent to those who are not decent to you.

Your thoughts return to the present as the judge enters the courtroom. You stand with the rest, the gavel comes down, and you sit. At your table is one other man, the prosecuting attorney, looking confident and condescending. You sit by yourself, expected to offer your own defense. The clerk steps forward and announces your name.

He begins by describing your crime: "He has broken the law of the land. He has been a source of trouble in the community because he has refused to obey the law that requires all to keep holy the rest day established by the United Nations. He has refused to perform his required work on Saturday. All the Christian churches as well as every other religion in the world are obeying the new law. He is breaking the law by teaching Bible prophecies that have nothing to do with the world of today".

The prosecuting attorney now begins his presentation. You listen carefully, your blood pressure rising at his mistaken ideas and so-called "evidence." You want to interrupt, but you can't; your heart beats faster, and you want to cry. What are they trying to do? Make you out to be a criminal? You've lived an honest, hard-working life all these years, but you're being portrayed as the lowest of the low. You are conscious of all the people sitting behind you. Are your relatives in the crowd? They know what kind of person you've always been; what are they thinking?

The judge shifts his position on the bench and looks down at the documents on his desk. He announces, "The Bible has been declared a mere work of literature and meant only to be read as a book of poetry and mythology." He appears nervous and impatient.

Finally, you are called to stand and testify in your own defense. You pray that you won't forget the angels by your side, and that you will remember the promise you've been given from Luke 21:12-15: "...before all these, they shall lay their hands on you, and persecute you, delivering you up to the synagogues, and into prisons, being brought before kings and rulers for my name's sake. And it shall turn to you for a testimony. Settle it therefore in your hearts, not to meditate before what ye shall answer; for I will give you mouth and wisdom, which all your adversaries shall not be able to gainsay nor resist."

And the promise from Matthew 10:17–20: "But beware of men: for they will deliver you up to the councils, and they will scourge you in their synagogues; and ye shall be brought before governors and kings for my sake, for a testimony against them and the Gentiles. But when they deliver you up, take no thought how or what ye shall speak; for it shall be given you in that same hour what ye shall speak. For it is not ye that speak, but the Spirit of your Father which speaketh in you."

You pray for the words that God has promised to give you. You speak distinctly so that all in the courtroom can understand, "I believe that Jesus Christ, the Son of God, came to this earth to save lost humanity, and when people accept Him as their Savior and Friend, they will love Him by obeying His commandments. Satan is a real being who hates God and every person, and seeks to steal, kill, and destroy. The Bible is true, every bit of it; it is the one and only Book, centered on Christ Jesus, that changes lives. It has power to transform hopeless drug addicts, alcoholics, cruel and violent human beings, into clean, upstanding, useful citizens. It's beyond doubt. It cannot be compared to any other book."

But you are met with a cacophony of voices from the audience. You look around you. All laugh at you, pointing their fingers, and it's some time before order is restored. Obviously, they've not seen such miracles happen, but you have. They've not heard of any such thing; it's something the news media does not present to the public.

The judge looks out over the courtroom, "Order!" he cries. His gavel commands order though his face tells another story. Justice has fallen in the streets. You have no friends in court—but One. The Holy Spirit is by your side. The Son of God went through the same trial two thousand years ago, only much, much worse, shedding His blood in your place. Your courage returns.

Eventually you are convicted of treason. You have dishonored your fellow man by refusing to unite with them on the issue of which day to keep holy, and for refusing to stop teaching the Bible. Such a simple thing has suddenly become a worldwide issue. There have been some who have pressed the subject for years without the general population knowing. The ancient church of the Middle Ages changed the day and it is the sign of its powerful rulership over the minds and hearts of the world's populace. The church head, who has been officially named as the political and spiritual leader of all the religions and nations of the world, has named Sunday as the day of family togetherness, church attendance, and restful fun. You know it's not merely a matter of which day to rest—it's a matter of worship.

You want to shout, "You know the Ten Commandments! They used to be posted in the lobby of this building!" The judge nods at the sergeant-at-arms.

How long? Of course, you knew that the sentence would be just as long as it takes for you to fit in. The judge's face by now has turned red, and with thundering voice declares the sentence.

You return his threatening stare. You conclude, as they lead you back to your cell, that the judge's anger only betrays his confusion. As you sit on your hard bunk, you hope that you have said the Lord's words. Even though they didn't give you much of a chance to say anything, you hope your witness will lead some to go search the scriptures (if there are any left), the original ones, and choose to follow the teachings of Christ.

Periodically, the guards will "interview" you, using "enhanced interrogation" that mirror the cruelty of the past. You are able to keep the information about the whereabouts of your friends, but it gets more and more difficult as you grow weaker. At this point, you don't know anyway. The food comes only sporadically now. You remember a certain Christian man, imprisoned for his faith with the state's intention of starving him to death. The man had been sustained by a cat outside the prison that would bring a slice of bread to his barred window every day. "I can stay faithful too, Lord, if You will make me strong," you say. You spend lonely hours going over the Bible verses you have memorized. *I wish I had memorized more of them*, you think. Your greatest concern is not your possible punishment, but whether you've done enough to convince your family.

Word has come to your cell that Christ has returned. You know that it is not Christ because the scriptures teach that He will come in the clouds with millions of angels, that He will not touch the ground, and that His loyal people will be caught up to meet Him in the air. This pseudo-Christ is walking the earth, crowds are following him, the newscasters interview him, and all the world rejoices that "Christ" has come. His voice is gentle; he looks just like the pictures of Him hanging on people's walls. This so-called "Messiah" heals the sick and suffering, makes fire come down from heaven, and transports people from place to place with a wave of his hand. He has convinced all the world that he indeed blessed all who rested and went to church faithfully every first day of the week. It was he who suggests getting rid of the hated sect in one night, because, he says, "Those people are the cause of God's fierce wrath!"

But, somehow, the world is going on just as before, except it's worse. There is still violence, wars are still killing thousands, and "business as usual" holds the attention of merchants and politicians.

Soon word comes in the news that the date of your execution has been set. Then it is that the public will be free to come in and execute, in their own ways, those who refused to obey "the law." Your first concern is for your wife. Where is she? Is she all right? She is always uppermost in your mind. Saturday midnight will be the "cutoff" hour. People can come in with their weapons and do what they please with their victims. Will the faithful ones be rescued as you have always believed they would be?

The next Sabbath is spent with overwhelming mixed emotions. Fears for yourself and for all your loved ones occupy your thoughts and emotions; yet gladness and relief prevail deep down in your innermost being.

You hope that your Divine Rescuer will arrive on time, but if He doesn't, then you say, like Job, "though worms destroy my body, yet in my flesh shall I see God." You hope that you have repented of everything you ever did that was hateful and wrong—so much. Your past sins and faults, neglects, and self-centeredness make you sink into hopeless agony. Then the next moment, you are cheered, knowing your sins have all been confessed and forgiven, and that you belong to the King of Kings who is on His way! You have put your faith in the only One who has saved you, and who can save you now.

As the eleventh hour arrives your heart pounds.

Suddenly the ground begins to rumble. You stand up in your cell. How will all this end? Soon, another rumble. The walls begin to crack, the barred gates rattle and fall from their iron hinges. Sliding doors tip and break from their frames. Hysterical shouts rend the air. Guards run here and there. Prisoners escape and climb over rubble, their pale faces shining with excitement. Through broken concrete and twisted metal, they rush into the street, bumping into the terrified guards as they climb over each other to freedom. You join them, knowing your redemption is near. You head in the direction you saw your wife take weeks ago.

There she is! You see her running toward you as the building collapses behind her. Your embrace lasts but a moment as all hell breaks loose. The citizens, with their weapons bent on your destruction, are now running this way and that, wildly shouting. "He's coming! He's coming!" Some crouch, crying in fear, "I don't want to see him! Hide me!"

You shout aloud, "This is our God! We have waited for Him and He will save us!"

As you enter the street, the sky blazes with fire. Above, a brilliant scene takes your breath away; it is of the great golden chest, the ark of the covenant, appearing in the heavens. Everyone looks in stunned silence as the great chest with golden angels atop opens for all to see inside. Two tables of stone are lifted by unseen hands from the chest for everyone to see. The Ten Commandments! And upon the fourth commandment, which says to keep the seventh day holy, shines a soft light. All who have hated that commandment cringe in sudden realization and fear.

The night sky shines radiant, brighter than sunshine. You look up. The King of Kings approaches closer and closer. Jesus, the true Messiah, comes in the clouds, clothed in super white garments, a glittering crown on His head. You see His eyes on you and thrill at the thought. Trumpets sound. Thousands, yes, millions of angels surrounding Him, sing joyful music you've never heard before. Most people try to hide or run away, but they are frozen in their tracks at the awesome sight.

And suddenly you both feel yourselves being lifted into the air. And as you look around, many, including your fellow believers, rise with you. You see your faithful parents, now resurrected from the grave. What a reunion! Down below the wicked shout for the rocks and mountains to cover them.

There are only two kinds of people now.

But that's the way it's always been.

There's no middle ground.

CONCLUSION

● ● ● ●

Prophecies found in Scripture that deal with the last days are rapidly ful-filling. Like the words of the ancient prophets that came to pass at the exact time, in the exact way, current national and world events prove the Bible to be true.

So be strong, reader. Take on new courage. The tragedies of the present will soon be over. Do what you can to help others and prepare yourself to live with God. Know that the devil, who is not a cartoon character after all, will get his reward, along with those who do his work.

And know too, that no matter how "good" we are, we'll never get to heaven on our own. It will take our dependence on the perfect merits of the Son of God to get us there.

Oh, and the cat who brought bread to the cell window turned out to belong to the warden and had taken his bread to the prisoner. Miracles happen every day.

Probably the ark made for God in the wilderness will never be found in spite of many attempts in the present and past. The tragedy of Bethsh-emesh would be repeated a thousand times over. The Lord knows what He's doing.

ONCE TO EVERY MAN AND NATION

Once to every man and nation comes the moment to decide,
In the strife of truth with falsehood, for the good or evil side;
Some great cause, God's new Messiah, offering each the bloom or blight,
And the choice goes by forever 'twixt that darkness and that light.
Then to side with truth is noble when we share her wretched crust,
Ere her cause bring fame and profit, and 'tis prosperous to be just;
Then it is the brave man chooses while the coward stands aside,
Till the multitude make virtue of the faith they had denied.
By the light of burning martyrs, Christ, thy bleeding feet we track,
Toiling up new Calvaries ever with the cross that turns not back;
New occasions teach new duties, time makes ancient good uncouth;
They must upward still and onward, who would keep abreast of truth.
Though the cause of evil prosper, yet 'tis truth alone is strong;
Though her portion be the scaffold, and upon the throne be wrong;
Yet that scaffold sways the future, and behind the dim unknown,
Standeth God within the shadow, keeping watch above His own.

James Russell Lowell

BIBLE REFERENCES FOR
MYSTERY OF THE GOLDEN CHEST

● ● ● ●

Chapter 1: Earth's Dilemma—How It All Started
(Genesis 3; Isaiah 14:12–14; Ezekiel 28:13–19; Revelation 12:7–9)

Chapter 2: The Refugee
(Exodus 2–20)

Chapter 3: God's Show and Tell
(Exodus 36–40)

Chapter 4: Destiny in Progress
(Numbers 20:7–12; Genesis 50:24–26; Numbers 27:18–23; Joshua 3)

Chapter 5: A Coal Snatched From the Burning
(Joshua 2, 6; Matthew 1:5; Hebrews 11:30–31)

Chapter 6: The Golden Mice
(1 Samuel 4–7)

Chapter 7: Uzzah
(2 Samuel 6:1–15; 1 Chronicles 13, 15)

Chapter 8: The Visit
(1 Kings 10:1–13; 2 Chronicles 9:1–12)

Chapter 9: Advice Rejected
(Jeremiah 37–39)

Chapter 10: History's Climax
(Matthew 27; Mark 15; Luke 23; John 19)

Chapter 11: The Two Priests
(Matthew 27:51; Mark 15:38; Luke 23:45; Hebrews 8–9)

Chapter 12: The Prison Break
(Matthew 28; Mark 16; Luke 24; John 20; Matthew 24:44)

Chapter 13: John the Revelator
(Matthew 20:20–23; Mark 10:35–39; Revelation 1:9–10; Revelation 11:19)

Chapter 14: Light in the Darkness—Hiram Edson
(Daniel 8:13, 14, 17; Leviticus 16; Isaiah 28:10; Hebrews 8–10; Revelation 10:8–11)

Chapter 15: The Rock That Changed a Little Girl's Life
(Joel 2:28; Amos 3:7; Isaiah 8:20; Revelation 12:17; 19:10; 2 Chronicles 20:20)

Chapter 16: The Two Laws
(Exodus 20: 1 John 3:4; Leviticus 1–17; Hebrews 9:13, 14; Revelation 22:14)

Chapter 17: Where Will You End Up?
(2 Timothy 2:21; Zephaniah 2:3; 1 Thessalonians 5:2–5; Revelation 21:3; 1 Corinthians 15:52)

CPSIA information can be obtained
at www.ICGtesting.com
Printed in the USA
FSHW021000140320
68008FS